ITIL® and the Software Lifec
Practical Strategy and Design P

Other publications by Van Haren Publishing

Van Haren Publishing (VHP) specializes in titles on Best Practices, methods and standards within IT and business management. These publications are grouped in the following series: *ITSM Library* (on behalf of ITSMF International), *Best Practice* and *IT Management Topics*. VHP is also publisher on behalf of leading companies and institutions, eg The Open Group, IPMA-NL, CA, Getronics, Pink Elephant. At the time of going to press the following books are available:

IT (Service) Management / IT Governance

ITSM, ITIL® V3 and ITIL® V2
Foundations of IT Service Management – based on ITIL V3
 (English and Dutch versions Autumn 2007, French, German, Japanese and Spanish editions: Winter 2007)
IT Service Management – An Introduction (English and Dutch versions Autumn 2007, French, German, Japanese and Spanish editions: Winter 2007)
IT Service Management based on ITIL V3 – A Pocket Guide
 (English and Dutch versions Autumn 2007, French, German, Japanese and Spanish editions: Winter 2007)
IT Service Management based on ITIL V3 – A Pocket Guide
 (English and Dutch versions Autumn 2007, French, German, Japanese and Spanish editions: Winter 2007)
Foundations of IT Service Management based on ITIL® (ITIL V2),
 (English, Dutch, French, German, Spanish, Japanese, Chinese, Danish, Italian, Korean, Russian, Arabic; also available as a CD-ROM)
Implementing Service and Support Management Processes (English)
IT Service Management - een samenvatting, 2de druk (Dutch)
Release and Control for IT Service Management, based on ITIL® - A Practitioner Guide (English)

ISO/IEC 20000
ISO/IEC 20000 - A Pocket Guide (English, Italian, German, Spanish, Portuguese)
ISO/IEC 20000 – An Introduction (English: Autumn 2007)
Implementing ISO/IEC 20000 (English: Autumn 2007)

ISO 27001 and ISO 17799
Information Security based on ISO 27001 and ISO 17799 - A Management Guide (English)
Implementing Information Security based on ISO 27001 and ISO 17799 - A Management Guide (English)

CobiT
IT Governance based on CobiT4® - A Management Guide (English, German)

IT Service CMM
IT Service CMM - A Pocket Guide (English)

ASL and BiSL
ASL - A Framework for Application Management (English, German)
ASL - Application Services Library - A Management Guide (English, Dutch)
BiSL - A Framework for Business Information Management (Dutch, English)
BiSL - Business information Services Library - A Management Guide (Dutch; English edition due Autumn 2007)

ISPL
IT Services Procurement op basis van ISPL (Dutch)
IT Services Procurement based on ISPL – A Pocket Guide (English)

IT Topics & Management instruments
De RfP voor IT-outsourcing (Dutch; English version due autumn 2007)
Decision- en Controlfactoren voor IT-Sourcing (Dutch)
Defining IT Success through the Service Catalog (English)
Frameworks for IT Management - An introduction
 (English, Japanese; German edition Autumn 2007)

Frameworks for IT Management – A Pocket Guide (Winter 2007)
Implementing leading standards for IT management (English, Dutch)
IT Service Management Best Practices, volumes 1, 2, 3 and 4 (Dutch)
ITSM from hell! / ITSM from hell based on Not ITIL (English)
ITSMP - The IT Strategy Management Process (English)
Metrics for IT Service Management (English)
Service Management Process Maps (English)
Six Sigma for IT Management (English)
Six Sigma for IT Management – A Pocket Guide (English)

MOF/MSF
MOF - Microsoft Operations Framework, A Pocket Guide (Dutch, English, French, German, Japanese)
MSF - Microsoft Solutions Framework, A Pocket Guide (English, German)

IT Architecture
TOGAF, The Open Group Architecture Framework – A Management Guide (English)
The Open Group Architecture Framework – 2007 Edition (English, official publication of TOG)
TOGAF™ Version 8 Enterprise Edition – Study Guide (English, official publication of TOG)
TOGAF™ Version 8 Enterprise Edition –Pocket Guide (English, official publication of TOG)

Quality Management

ISO 9000
ISO 9001:2000 - The Quality Management Process (English)

EFQM
The EFQM excellence model for Assessing Organizational Performance – A Management Guide (English)

Project/Programme/Risk Management

ICB
NCB – Nederlandse Competence Baseline (Dutch on behalf of IPMA-NL)
Handboek Projectmanagement voor IPMA-C en IPMA-D (Dutch, early 2008)

PRINCE2™
Project Management based on PRINCE2™- Edition 2005 (English, Dutch, German)
PRINCE2™ - A No Nonsense Management Guide (English)
PRINCE2™ voor opdrachtgevers – Management Guide (Dutch)

MINCE®
MINCE® – A Framework for Organizational Maturity (English)

MSP
Programme Management based on MSP (English, Dutch)
Programme Management based on MSP - A Management Guide (English)

M_o_R
Risk Management based on M_o_R - A Management Guide (English)

For the latest information on VHP publications, visit our website: www.vanharen.net

ITIL® and the Software Lifecycle: Practical Strategy and Design Principles

Brian Johnson
John Higgins

Colophon

Title:	ITIL® and the Software Lifecycle: Practical Strategy and Design Principles
Authors:	Brian Johnson and John Higgins
Advisers:	Richard Warden, Helge Scheil, Alan Nance
Reviewers:	Brian Hughes, John Kampman, Malcolm Fry
Editors:	Nancy Hinich, Jayne Wilkinson, Nisha Patel
Publisher:	Van Haren Publishing, Zaltbommel, www.vanharen.net
ISBN:	9789087530495
Print:	First edition, first impression, August 2007 First edition, second impression October 2007 First edition, third impression January 2008
Layout and design:	C02 Premedia, Amersfoort – NL
Printer:	Wilco, Amersfoort - NL

© Brian Johnson and John Higgins 2007

For further information about Van Haren Publishing, please send an email to info@vanharen.net

Brian Johnson and John Higgins have asserted their right to be identified as the Authors of this work under the Copyright, Designs and Patents Act, 1988.

Although every effort has been taken to compose this publication with the utmost care, the Authors, Editors and Publisher cannot accept any liability for damage caused by possible errors and/or incompleteness within this publication. Any mistakes or omissions brought to the attention of the Publisher will be corrected in subsequent editions.

All rights reserved. No part of this publication can be reproduced in any form in print, photo print., microfilm or any other means without written permission by the publisher.
ITIL® is a Registered Trade Mark, and a Registered Community Trade Mark of the Office of Government Commerce, and is Registered in the U.S. Patent and Trademark Office.
IT Infrastructure Library® is a Registered Trade Mark of the Office of Government Commerce.
PRINCE® is a Registered Trade Mark and a Registered Community Trade Mark of the Office of Government Commerce, and is Registered in the U.S. Patent and Trademark Office.
PRINCE2™ is a Trade Mark of the Office of Government Commerce
SSADM® is a Registered Trade Mark of the Office of Government Commerce.

This book covers best practice as described in all three versions of ITIL, and treats ITIL in generic, rather than version-specific terms. Where a particular version is applicable, it is clearly specified in the text.

Acknowledgements

The Authors would like to thank and gratefully acknowledge the following individuals for their help with this book:

Thanks to Richard Warden, Helge Scheil and Alan Nance for their contributions to the book, and to Brian Hughes, John Kampman and Malcolm Fry for reviewing this work.

Editorial scrutiny and sanity checking thanks to Nancy Hinich, our Editor-in-Chief, Jayne Wilkinson and Nisha Patel.

WE ARE MACMILLAN. CANCER SUPPORT

All author royalties* from this work will be contributed to MacMillan Cancer Support* (Registered charity no. 261017).

*Paid to Macmillan Cancer Support Trading Limited, a wholly owned subsidiary of Macmillan Cancer Support, to which it gives all of its taxable profits.

Foreword

As someone who has been part of the IT industry for the last 30 years, I have watched IT mature from essentially a bookkeeping function to one that is at the heart of modern business processes. There are few companies today that don't have some reliance on Information Technology, and an increasing number that are completely dependent upon it. Therefore, it is surprising that for all the importance of IT, there has been so little focus on the IT processes *per se*; the methodologies, tools and techniques that people use to build, manage and secure IT.

ITIL® has been instrumental in energizing this discussion, especially in the last few years, when auditors and regulators have highlighted the need for a company to follow good IT practices, encouraging IT managers to look more closely at IT processes. As IT has matured as a discipline, so too has ITIL, moving from its initial focus on operations management to a broader focus on interfacing with applications development and wider service management. At the end of the day, this is very healthy ... and so too is a continued debate about theory versus practice.

Books such as this serve to help people understand how to better apply process discipline to their environment, so they can ultimately deliver a higher quality of service at a lower cost to the business. Ultimately, that's what IT is for ... using technology to automate business processes, and allowing people to innovate on top of those processes, to deliver a higher quality service or product. I am proud that we at CA can be part of that value chain, by helping ensure that we provide people, tools and processes to transform the way our customers manage Information Technology.

John A Swainson
President and CEO
CA, Inc.

Table of Contents

1　Management Summary — 1
　1.1　Where Do We Start? — 2
　1.2　Co-ordination — 2
　1.3　Benefits — 4
　1.4　Who Is The Customer? — 5

2　A Common Ground — 9
　2.1　Aligning Development and Operations Teams — 9

3　IT Service Design: The Fundamentals — 11
　3.1　Purpose of this book — 11
　3.2　What is an Application/Software Lifecycle? — 11
　3.3　What is Application Lifecycle Support? — 12
　3.4　A Joint Approach — 13
　3.5　What Is Provided — 13
　3.6　Who May be Interested? — 13
　3.7　Coverage — 14

4　Planning for Application Lifecycle Support — 17
　4.1　Concepts — 17
　4.2　Lifecycle model descriptions — 17
　　4.2.1　Introduction — 17
　　4.2.2　The Waterfall Model — 19
　　4.2.3　The Spiral Model — 21
　　4.2.4　Agile and Rapid Prototyping Models — 24
　　4.2.5　Issues — 31
　　4.2.6　Summary — 31

5　Assessment and Selection of Lifecycle Models — 33
　5.1　Introduction — 33
　5.2　Attributes — 34
　　5.2.1　Service type — 34
　　5.2.2　Uncertainty of requirements — 34
　　5.2.3　Interfaces with other services — 35
　　5.2.4　Annual Change traffic — 35
　　5.2.5　Timeframes for development — 36
　　5.2.6　Service size — 36
　5.3　Assessment of Existing Models — 36
　　5.3.1　Selection of a Lifecycle Model — 37
　　5.3.2　Modification of a lifecycle model — 38

6	**Interfaces with Major Management and Planning Activities**	**39**
	6.1 Introduction	39
	6.2 Role of the IT planning Unit	41
	6.3 IT Service Design Team (ITSDT)	41
	6.4 Using Lifecycle Models in ITSDT	44
	6.5 Plans	45
	6.6 Relationship with other IT related functions	45
	6.6.1 Quality Management	45
	6.6.2 Security Management	46
	6.6.3 Risk Management	46
	6.6.4 Compliance	46
	6.7 Cost/benefit Assessment	46
	6.8 Organizational Issues	47
7	**Planning for Service Design**	**49**
	7.1 Introduction	49
	7.1.1 Appoint an IT Service Co-ordinator	49
	7.1.2 Assessment and selection of Lifecycle Models	51
	7.1.3 Core issues	51
	7.1.4 Major Considerations	51
8	**Using a Lifecycle Model to Plan for Operational Management Intervention**	**55**
	8.1 Identification and Management of Interfaces	55
	8.2 Extensions to models	56
	8.3 Generic Models	56
	8.4 Using a lifecycle model to plan for software maintenance	57
	8.4.1 Operational management and software maintainability	57
	8.4.2 Operational management and the maintenance process	58
	8.5 Application to existing services	59
	8.5.1 Documenting Operational management activities	60
	8.6 Change Management	62
	8.7 Capacity planning and structured methods	64
	8.8 Impact	65
9	**Dependencies**	**67**
	9.1 Related Factors	68
	9.2 IT Service - Co-ordinator	69
	9.3 Staffing Requirements	69
	9.4 Organizing Staff	70
	9.5 When to begin	70
	9.5.1 Pilot Projects	71
	9.5.2 Existing Projects	71

10 Embedding — 73
- 10.1 Actions — 73
- 10.2 Running a pilot project — 73
- 10.3 Dependencies — 74
- 10.4 People involved — 75
- 10.5 When to take action — 75

11 Review and Audit — 77
- 11.1 Actions — 77
- 11.2 Effectiveness and efficiency review — 77
- 11.3 Project Review — 78
- 11.4 Review of the pilot project — 78
- 11.5 Other Reviews — 79
- 11.6 Responsibility — 79

12 Benefits and Costs: The Good, the Bad and the Ugly — 81
- 12.1 Benefits of a Pilot Project — 81
- 12.2 Long-term benefits — 81
- 12.3 Costs — 82
- 12.4 Possible Problems — 83

13 Technology Support — 85
- 13.1 Tools for the IT Service Co-ordinator — 85
- 13.2 Tools for Operational Management — 86
- 13.3 Tools for Development & Maintenance Teams — 86
- 13.4 Tools for Project & Portfolio Management — 86

Annex One: Definitions and Abbreviations — 89

Annex Two: Summary of the Principal IT Service Design Process Steps — 93

Annex Three: Procedures for Application to Existing Services — 95
- Introduction — 95
  - Document and assess the current situation — 95
  - Enhancing strategies — 96
  - Improvement work required for a new lifecycle strategy — 97

Annex Four: Impact on Specific Infrastructure Management Activities — 99
- Introduction — 99
- The Business Perspective series — 99
- Customer Liaison — 101
- Planning and Control for IT Services — 101
- Quality Management for IT Services (QMFITS) — 102

Managing Facilities Management	102
Cost/ Financial Management for IT Services	104
Service Level Management (SLM)	104
Capacity Management	105
Disaster Recovery and Business Continuity Planning	106
Availability Management	107
Configuration Management and Change Management	108
Incident and Problem Management	110
Service Desk	110
Computer Operations Management	111
Unattended Operating	113
Testing Software for Operational Use	113
Release (Software Control and Distribution) Management	114
Continuous improvement (the Plan Do Check Act Cycle)	114
Security	115
Network Services Management (Information and Communications Technology-ICT)	116
Service Catalog Management	116

Annex Five: Theory into Practice   **117**

Annex Six: References   **121**

CHAPTER 1 Management Summary

The aim of this book is to provide guidance around the adoption of best practices when designing IT services in your organization, through integrating processes for the development of software assets with those published in industry frameworks such as the IT Infrastructure Library (ITIL®) and ISO20000.

The method adopted in this book reflects a shift of emphasis to a business driven approach, where IT service design is elevated to be the logical starting point for implementations. The industry may now be ready for this approach, with many organizations achieving the high levels of maturity required, in order to enable customers, application developers and operations managers to work together. In other words, the underlying processes, most often centered on service support techniques such as incident, problem and change management, have been the focus of process improvements for many years, and some organizations are now ready to embed the service delivery processes necessary in order to facilitate such a shift of emphasis.

The concept of IT service design is certainly not a new one, but in the past, organizations have had to focus first on improving the underlying *operational* processes which act as the foundation of the IT enterprise.

Industry Best Practice guidance, such as ITIL® and ISO20000 describes most processes, although certain aspects could be given greater prominence:

- security management
- application management
- software change management
- IT asset management
- a close mapping of project management and resource management

The lack of detail within these elements poses a problem when an organization decides to move to an IT service design model, because quality, stability and availability of an IT service are determined by all of the lifecycles that flow in and out of the service lifecycle; for example, IT Assets have their own lifecycle from the time of requisition through to retirement, and this overlaps at predetermined points of the *overall* service lifecycle; so it is clear that impacts from one, have a 'domino effect' on the others.

This title presents readers with an approach to software development that builds on established processes and also achieves a goal of better alignment of IT services within business needs.

1.1 Where Do We Start?

With a closer co-operation between customers of IT services, operational managers and software developers, the ultimate goal of ensuring the provision of quality IT services becomes that of meeting the demands of the business.

This book reinforces the many benefits obtained from the adoption of structured methods of software development (such as building in security and governance, and compliance objectives such as maintainability, quality and segregation of duties), and extends those benefits by promoting a culture in which the needs of the business are completely met by a close co-operation throughout the lifecycle of Software Development.

1.2 Co-ordination

What is the role of IT Service Management? Figure 1 presents a simplified picture:

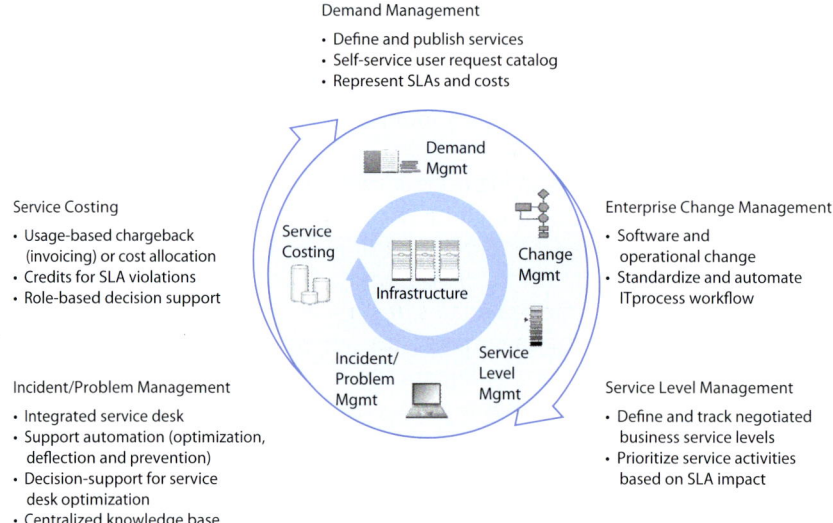

Figure 1: Service Lifecycle Management

In any IT environment, such as the one illustrated above, customer demands are met through the provision of IT services.

By definition, an IT service is a collection of technology-based elements (hardware and software) and low technology-based artifacts (documents, facilities), which exist to fulfill a business need.

The provision of IT services can be met through:

- the development of new services (alignment to business need)
- testing new software (quality and adherence to requirements)
- the running and maintenance of live IT services (stability/availability)
- continual alignment with changing business requirements (enhancement)
- maintenance and upgrading of software and hardware (future proofing/protection)

When operational managers are appropriately involved in the stages of service development, they can ensure that the requirements are met for running and maintaining the proposed service as part of the *delivery* of IT services.

The collective activities of customer involvement, software development and maintenance can be co-ordinated as a single approach. This approach can then be labeled in a number of ways, including 'application lifecycle support', 'service design support', or 'technical co-ordination'. Whatever label this co-ordinated approach is given, the ultimate goal should be to create an organizational unit that is capable of understanding the use of IT applications, in a customer environment that can liaise effectively with all domains; domains that encompass systems analyst/developers, database administrators, programmers, testing units, technical support experts, operations, and most importantly, consumers.

IT provides opportunities to incorporate good practices at an early stage of development, to reduce running costs and manage change throughout the application lifecycle, from design through to decommissioning.

Essentially, as a result, a long-term view is taken of the development, maintenance and enhancement of software. It is important that software developers and operational managers are aware that IT services provided to customers are dependent on **both** parties understanding the customers' requirement, understanding mutual constraints and working together to deliver the best possible IT services.

Developers will continue to embrace their preferred method of application requirement gathering and design (whether SSADM®, DSDM, LSDM or Yourdon, some of which are discussed later in this book); but they will educate their operations colleagues on the critical information required from them, in order to take a co-ordinated approach to the application lifecycle. This enables the inclusion of operational management requirements at the design and development stages, to ensure that legacy services are correctly assessed and decommissioned, and, of course, also to ensure that the IT services *delivered* are more efficient, that quality is inbuilt, that regulatory issues are addressed and that services are easier to maintain.

Adopting this co-ordinated approach helps IT to deliver services that have been *designed* to meet service level requirements, while creating opportunity to consider new technological solutions, and hence re-engineer the business processes more effectively when necessary. It then becomes possible to deliver and maintain services which enable and encourage changing business objectives over an extended economic life, and reinforces security, maintainability, compliance and quality requirements, at an early stage.

Application lifecycle support co-ordinates operational management with Development and Maintenance, so that services are not only designed for maintainability, but are *supported* fully throughout their cycles. This approach is not a new one; however, the caveat to this option is the requirement for a high degree of organizational maturity in all IT domains and for a 'change embracing' culture.

It is not easy to embed these types of demands in an organization focused solely on a process approach. The issues have to be addressed around organizational readiness (most organizations are barely in control of incident lifecycle management) and the cultural hurdle of persuading applications developers that a service management method has merit, even within their own domain. IT Service Management, as described in this publication, is about planning for, addressing and actioning these cultural hurdles, by involving and co-ordinating development, maintenance and operational management teams, to bridge the gaps that typically may have stalled earlier process improvement projects and programs.

1.3 Benefits

In the long run, it is the *value* of the IT service provision that is most crucial. Value is determined by quality, as it relates to cost. A major cost of IT continues to be software maintenance. Other critical issues to the business include agility and flexibility for implementing changes.

In today's climate, it is essential to build in local (national) and international regulatory compliance criteria, to enable IT to address such issues more effectively. Here again, best practices will be required from a range of frameworks, such as ITIL®, ISO20000, COSO (Committee of Sponsoring

Organizations of the Treadway Commission) and CobiT (Control Objectives for Information and Related Technology).

Using both structured methods and lifecycle support processes enables security, compliance and quality to be built into software products, thereby reducing overall maintenance costs and improving the quality of delivered services to customers. Their use also facilitates the building-in of interoperability, portability of systems and openness through standards.

The costs of involving IT service customers and operational managers in software development will be more than offset by reduced costs in providing and maintaining IT services over their lifetime. Additionally, the business customer benefits from the provision of more reliable and flexible IT services. Of course, none of these benefits can be realized unless the organization tracks the current cost of service provision effectively, and continues to track costs over the lifetime of the projects which are needed to maintain the quality of services.

A co-ordinated approach to service design and support contributes to the economic provision of IT services by:

- significantly improving the communications between IT groups who, traditionally, have worked in silo units
- reducing overall running costs of development and maintenance work (the maintenance part of the lifecycle is the major lifecycle cost and presents a considerable opportunity for overall cost savings)
- improving the overall quality of procedures and productivity of IT, thereby reducing problems when introducing new services into a live environment
- enabling IT services to contribute to better economic appraisal of services and improved estimation of the total service costs to the customer
- providing IT project managers and service managers with key performance indicators (KPIs)
- providing audit trails through processes which are linked together and are cohesive
- enabling co-ordinated planning for security, quality and compliance throughout the entire service lifecycle
- enabling the identification of trends in service management which will assist in the planning of future services (interoperability, portability, open-systems)

1.4 Who Is The Customer?

One of the reasons that development and operations domains have differed in approaches is because operations typically *provide* IT services to development teams. However, testing environments and development

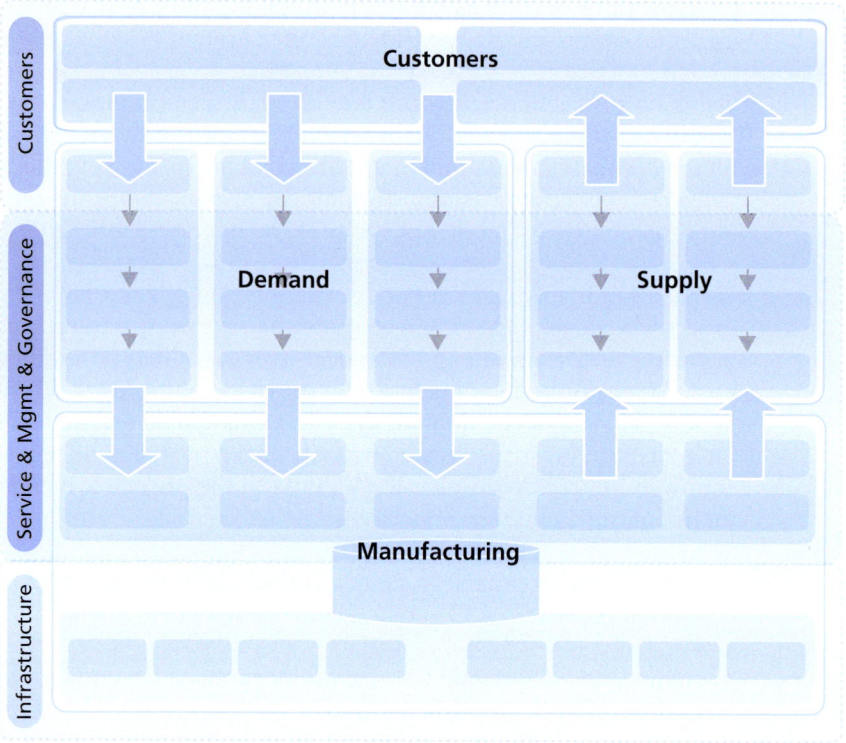

Figure 2: Business Service Factory

environments are **both** IT services, and before operations can truly embrace IT service design, they must first establish a good relationship with the key customers involved in the provision of applications to the business. Figure 2 is an illustration of the customers for whom IT must provide services.

Business customers are largely (although unfairly, from an IT perspective) not interested in IT service provision from the operational standpoint. Their view of IT is filtered through their vision of how useful the applications are that they use day-to-day, and by the availability of those applications. As a result of this, IT service design can only really be established within the context of that common perception. And IT service design will be different, depending on the customer; one size will not fit all.

Business requirements must translate into functional requirements, which in turn, must translate into the application architecture; transparency is the key, and this transparency can only be achieved in the design of the IT services, up front.

Designing robust IT services requires that the importance of the ITIL service delivery processes is elevated, because of their role in the initial stages of development design, and therefore IT *service* design. It is the objective of this book to provide guidance around these necessary collective activities and stages of lifecycle management, encompassing operations, development and maintenance.

CHAPTER 2 A Common Ground

This book stresses the need for communication between customers of IT services, software developers and operational managers; it stresses the need for each to understand the requirements of the other, and how these requirements are managed using lifecycles; essentially, a common ground for traditionally 'siloed' units. The book describes how adopting the use of lifecycles will assist in the planning and monitoring of projects which meet business objectives and facilitate the design of robust, business-focused IT services. It will demonstrate that IT service design cannot be successfully undertaken by the operations side alone, which has traditionally been the focus for ITIL related projects.

2.1 Aligning Development and Operations Teams

This book focuses on culture change, and changing the way people work, rather than on introducing radically new activities. New activities (considered new for those unfamiliar with structured development methods, ITIL version 1 or the use of lifecycles) are discussed, but the activities can be, for the most part, carried out using existing staff and by adaptation of the current IT organization.

Focusing on IT service design is not a new idea; it has been possible to work in this manner for decades, but the focus for most of the IT market to date has been elsewhere, due to the number of stakeholders required, and the level of cultural change required for successful implementations.

A probable exception to the general rule of relatively minor organizational change being required, is the creation of an IT service design team, to liaise between the various IT domains; of necessity this will be an *authoritative* team, comprised of senior managers and middle managers of good technical and business background with exceptional people skills.

The introduction of lifecycle support procedures often necessitates new ways of working in an organization. There are a number of key principles:

- Effective infrastructure support requires that operational managers communicate with software developers and have knowledge of the lifecycle stages of software development and maintenance.
- ITIL roles need to be elevated from being service *support* centric to service *delivery* focused.
- Developers must be consulted throughout the entire service lifecycle in order for ITIL roles to assist in the design of IT services focused on the business.

- Management of the introduction of new software services to the operational environment needs to be planned and implemented so that service levels can be maintained in a cost-effective manner, for consistency and understanding.
- Software developers and software maintainers should use the same management structures, methods and tools, and have the same interactions with the operational managers.
- Maintenance tasks must be planned, designed and implemented at every stage of the development process.

CHAPTER 3 IT Service Design: The Fundamentals

3.1 The Purpose of this Book

A major aim of this book is to demystify the role of frameworks across all IT domains, so that all parties can focus on what really matters: *service to the customer*. There is no single framework or method that will fix *all* of the issues faced by IT, so this title approaches the subject by applying the most pertinent information from a variety of different sources.

Another theme of this book is to provide operational management with an understanding of the concept of lifecycles; to explain how lifecycles can be used to build good practices for operational managers, and how the lifecycle support processes can improve the quality of *delivered* IT services to customers.

The key message is that software developers and operational managers need to communicate, and, where possible, co-ordinate planning for IT service delivery. It is not the aim of the book to take over the responsibility for selection of software lifecycles for development work, nor is the message of this book one of interference. Software developers must retain their current responsibilities for lifecycle selection and associated process modeling. It is simply recommended that other key personnel (IT service customers and operational managers) should participate in a co-ordinated approach to the overall planning processes.

3.2 What is an Application/Software Lifecycle?

A simple definition of the word 'lifecycle' is *the time period between starting and finishing an activity of some sort*; however, an 'application lifecycle' (or software lifecycle - the terms are synonymous) is usually defined in a more complex (or comprehensive) way.

An application lifecycle is a representation of the complete lifetime of a software development (which will become a service or component of a service delivered to a customer), from initial conception to final decommissioning (or, using extreme programming dialect, 'death'!). A projected lifecycle can be used for planning purposes. It is the sequence of stages through which software systems pass. It is not possible to manage the stages of a lifecycle without thinking in terms of a project. The lifecycle covers the following stages:

- the starting point - when the software specification is first written
- the development lifecycle - the period of time that begins with the decision to develop a software product and ends when an acceptable product is delivered for implementation as part of live IT services (this time period includes testing and acceptance of the software)
- software maintenance - the modification of a software product after delivery, in order to correct faults, improve performance or other attributes (enhancement), or to adapt the product to a changed environment
    - decommissioning - the point at which the software is no longer useful to the organization

3.3 What is Application Lifecycle Support?

Application lifecycle support is a co-ordinated approach between developers and operational management, through the activities of supporting software development from its initial design and, ultimately, to its decommissioning and disposal.

The approach is co-ordinated by using a lifecycle model which indicates the complete life of a service and provides the opportunity to identify the interfaces to operational management. This method was discussed in version 1 of ITIL by authors Brian Johnson and Richard Warden; then, as now, few IT organizations were really sufficiently mature to make full use of those concepts.

Version 3 of ITIL revisits this premise as a 'new' concept by focusing on service design. The issues are no different, and version 3 does not provide any new insight into the organizational change that is required for successful co-ordination.

Many organizations use some kind of lifecycle model, but often they only describe *part* of the overall lifecycle, and do not account for all the interactions that may be required between customers, developers, maintainers and operational managers. Assessment and selection of the most suitable lifecycle model for IT systems development means that:

- developers use lifecycle models which are appropriate to the IT services they are developing
    - the issues of software maintenance are properly addressed
    - during the development phase, software maintenance is managed and controlled with the same rigor employed in design of applications
    - the operational management services required to support a lifecycle model are properly planned and implemented throughout the life of the service

3.4 A Joint Approach

A joint approach requires careful planning to marry the efforts of operational managers, software developers and customers of IT services. Lifecycle modeling is used to identify and document every stage in the life of an IT service and the associated interactions with operational activities. Further, a recognized method of managing the entire project is in place. This book provides IT service managers with a description of the infrastructure requirements for planning and implementing a lifecycle model which covers all stages of a service life, from project initiation to final decommissioning, involving all relevant units, collaboratively.

3.5 What Is Provided

Within this book, guidance is provided for:

- lifecycle modeling and task description
- planning the infrastructure support for new software projects and existing services
- incorporating maintenance requirements into the software development process
- phasing of the implementation of new procedures necessary to facilitate co-operation between operational managers, software developers and customers of IT services

Clearly, future development projects will provide the most cost-effective opportunities to introduce lifecycle support (or *service design* if you prefer to adopt version 3 vernacular); wherever possible, guidance is also given on the application of these techniques to existing services. Only you can decide if the approach is more suitable than the process centric approach of version 2, and the major hurdle will be acceptance by applications management that ITIL has any role in their domain.

This book is not intended to define one prescriptive solution. Every organization will need to develop its own approach (because different lifecycles will be used, sometimes multiple lifecycles because of multiple projects), that can be adopted and adapted to suit individual circumstances.

3.6 Who May be Interested?

This book is primarily intended for operational planners and operational managers, who will need to understand the concepts, planning issues and procedures which need to be co-ordinated. Application development managers may be interested, if they are familiar with the Application Services Library (ASL is a library initiated by the Dutch Ministry of

Defense), or looking to implement the Best Practices described within ITIL® and ISO/IEC20000.

The book should also be of value to:

- IT development project managers; they will need to know how to work with an integrated approach to a project or a program of related projects to provide IT services
- Application systems analysts, designers, developers and maintainers, because they will need to know about the procedures and how they interface to related activities
- IT service designers

The authors of this title encourage and urge readers to adapt the generic recommendations within this title to the needs of their individual businesses wherever possible: there is an over reliance, a dependence even, on templates that become a poor substitute for creative teamwork, and this should be discouraged.

The book should be of interest to those customers who buy or use IT services, and who will gain an understanding of the benefits of the approach in improving the quality of the IT services they receive.

3.7 Coverage

As mentioned above, the principles of IT service design provide a bridge between operational management and the development and maintenance activities. In particular, it covers:

- project planning (for an individual project or a program of projects); it is not however, a substitute for a project management method (PRINCE2™ or the Project Management Institute's PMI)
- planning for software development and maintenance
- planning for operational management and operations

The book addresses the needs of in-house software development and does *not* include guidance about:

- packaged software
- software developed externally by a third party

Where an organization retains control of the operations and delivery of IT services while offering software development to an external supplier, a good proportion of the information in this book will be pertinent to planning for the impact of software delivery on the IT infrastructure. In such instances, an organization should be assured by the third party that software development is undertaken using accepted and preferably structured methods. This is because the cost of maintaining software is considerable and the cost can be reduced by designing software with maintainability in mind, so that the software runs efficiently on the existing IT infrastructure and is easily adaptable to any foreseeable changes to it.

The organization may decide to specify that third party software development should conform to independent standards. Again, to emphasize the issue, the book does not address in detail how to *implement* the procedures outlined. This is because IT environments differ in their composition and the possible interfaces between infrastructure management, software developers and maintainers are numerous. The book centers on the explanation of the concepts of lifecycle support and the procedures which can be presented as generalized guidance. It does cover an essential organizational change that has benefited a number of organizations that have used this approach.

In terms of the IT infrastructure, close co-operation with software developers and maintainers will have an impact on many of the operational management functions. The book discusses how specific operational management services may be affected in a number of ways, including the selection of software technologies and tools, and the use of project and quality management systems.

Incidentally, *all* of the ITIL® processes and functions are impacted by adoption of the decision to map application development; the most important mappings are discussed later in the book within Annex Four.

CHAPTER 4 Planning for Application Lifecycle Support

4.1 Concepts

This section explains the concepts that underpin lifecycle support:

- how the application lifecycle interfaces with other management and planning activities
- background on lifecycle models, and how they are used to plan lifecycle support activities and support the design of IT service provision
- the relationship with other operational management activities
- the issues that need to be considered when adopting lifecycle support concepts

4.2 Lifecycle Model Descriptions

4.2.1 Introduction

Lifecycle models are used to describe all of the stages through which software passes. They are used as the basis for both management and technical control. For management purposes, they identify all of the stages and activities that need to be resourced, scheduled and controlled in projects. For technical purposes, they help to identify the types of activities, and the methods, skills and technologies needed to execute them. In this respect there needs to be a clear mapping to project management.

This need for mapping to project management, poses a possible dilemma; the advice herein must be enforced so that the operational activities are understood and addressed in the development lifecycle. It can be difficult to impose some of the accepted principles within IT Service Management on a project management team working within the guidelines of a completely different framework. It is suggested then, that the IT service design team (see Chapter Six) should sit between these teams, to ensure both domains plan IT services with the customer in mind.

Many lifecycle models have been developed to meet the needs of different types of designing services and systems. A critical factor for successful IT service development and maintenance is choosing the right model. This is discussed in Chapter Five.

This section describes the following lifecycle models and their characteristics:

- waterfall
- spiral
- agile
- rapid prototyping

It is likely that experienced software developers would use a combination of lifecycle models in any given project. Customers of IT services and operational managers should look to software developers for their expertise and advice.

Care should be taken to differentiate between lifecycle models and methods. For example, the waterfall model is often applied to commercial developments. There are several sets of methods available to implement this model, such as Structured Systems Analysis and Design Method (SSADM), Learmonth Structured Development Method (LSDM) and Yourdon. A set of methods may not implement all stages within a model (eg some cover the analysis and design stages, but not implementation and maintenance). However, with common sense, each of the methods can be applied to a wide range of lifecycle models.

Once more, experienced software developers will be expected to provide guidance. ITIL does not address software development; it is not written by developers and therefore it is not the starting point for Application Service Design. It is stating the obvious, but the starting point is within applications and hence, it is imperative that applications management is allowed to drive analysis and design with the support of the operations side of IT.

To promote co-operation between customers of IT services, infrastructure management and software developers and maintainers, lifecycle models are being used more extensively. This approach is only successful when owned and driven through development, as it needs to center around the subject matter expertise (the application itself). Using the lifecycle models as the reference point, it is easy to link into the overarching project lifecycle.

However, there is a common deficiency in most models. They describe the design and development stages well, but leave maintenance either undefined, or as a single stage with no detailed definition. It is, for this reason, that the book concentrates on the enhancement of models, both to consider the maintainability requirements of operational management, and to define the maintenance stage in detail. Further useful guidance can be found in the ASL.

4.2.2 The Waterfall Model

None of the lifecycle models we mention are proprietary to ITIL; indeed ITIL has no relevance in the domains in which they are used. However, knowledge of how developers use the models is useful to the ITIL practitioner, to allow them to work in conjunction with development to design IT services that are less problematic to maintain. The waterfall model considers maintenance as on-going development, and wherever possible, applies the same stages with their corresponding operational management involvement.

The waterfall lifecycle model illustrated in Figure 3 is the most commonly used model and it is very common to see it utilised within commercial and government systems. Many software methods, such as SSADM, LSDM and Yourdon use this model as their base, and provide techniques for performing a part, any or all of the lifecycle stages.

Obviously, involvement of the operations side can be integrated, but this creates another dilemma; by far the majority of organizations looking to operate within ITIL® or ISO/IEC frameworks are still getting service support processes under control; however, the real benefit of a service design intervention comes with the discussion of the impact of new applications (maybe one-to-one with 'a service', but keep in mind that some applications will be run together, to form a service) on IT availability, costs and capacity. These are the service delivery processes that are largely absent or immature in many organizations today.

The major strength of this model is that it describes feedback loops between successive stages. The premise is to reduce potential rework required, by minimizing feedback through some of the stages. Early stages must be completed before later stages can begin. In other words, the requirements and design stages have to be fully documented before coding and integration can commence.

This style of working is appropriate for many commercial systems, but for interactive or end-user software, the waterfall model is often less suitable, as the requirements and design cannot always be completed before coding and testing takes place. And this, once again, creates an issue for those attempting to instantiate a service design approach; if developers cannot discuss requirements until coding is begun, the ability for the operations side to become appropriately involved, becomes limited. What is often required is a model which supports prototyping as a means of developing and refining requirements (ie iterative development).

Iterative development provides the best opportunity to participate, however, do not underestimate the impact on operational resources (one of the reasons for recommending IT service design as the go-between).

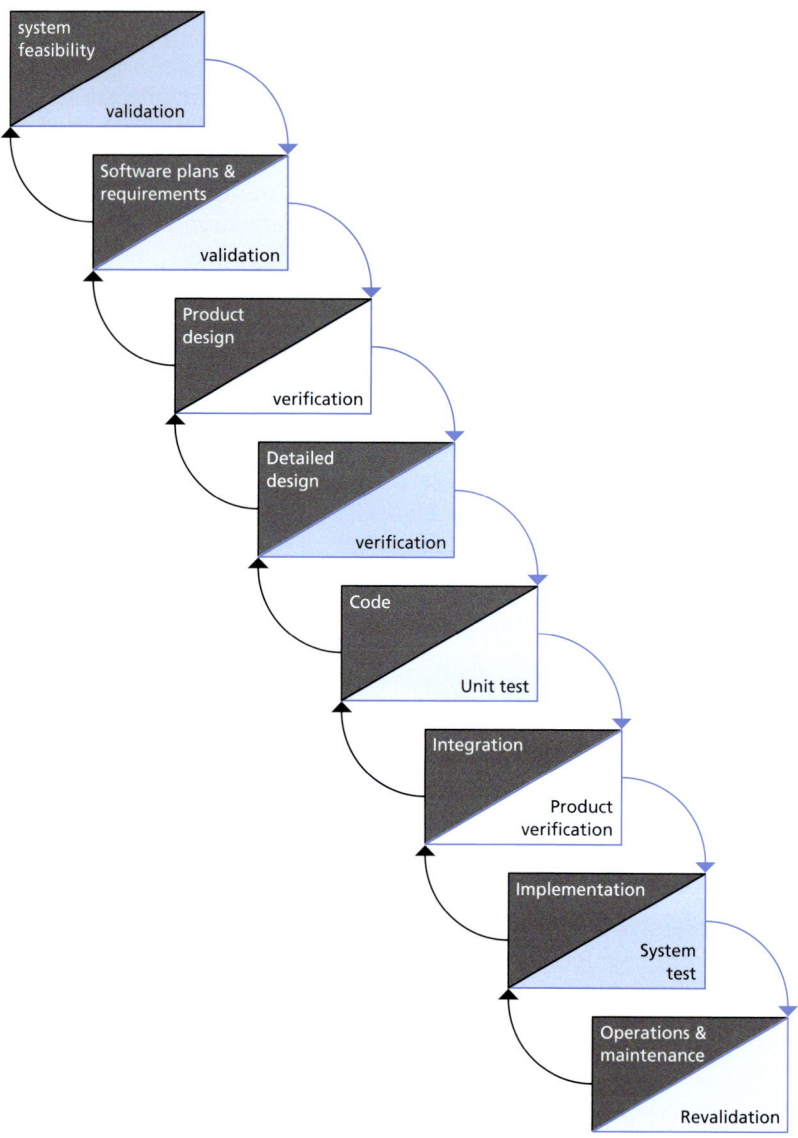

Figure 3: The Waterfall Lifecycle Model (originally attributed to Royce)

In summary then, from the operational management viewpoint, the waterfall model provides a good basis for planning operational support during development, due to its well defined, sequential stages. Unfortunately it does not describe the on-going maintenance stages well. It is better integrated with the (currently) under-resourced service delivery processes and therefore requires both model enhancements and more mature operational organizations, if the model is to be used for planning the involvement of operational management.

4.2.3 The Spiral Model

The usual depiction of the Barry Boehm spiral lifecycle model is an illustration of four spirals (described as whorls or phases), each comprising the stages:

- determine options, objectives and constraints
- evaluate options and resolve risks, using prototypes
- perform a stage of development - often preceded by some simulations, models and benchmarks
- plan for the next spiral phases

The spiral model is a generic model, from which the waterfall model, and others, can be created, by omitting or adding activities. To demonstrate this, the spiral model is given in generic terms, so that it is easier to compare with other models; the four phases of each and every spiral are described as follows:

- Initiation - takes place when a spiral whorl or phase is initiated.
- Risk assessment - the evaluation of alternatives and risk resolution.
- Development - the actual development stages performed during that spiral whorl.
- Planning - the planning of the next phase after the validation of one spiral whorl.

It is important to remember that between the planning stage at the end of one phase, and the initiation of the next phase, there is a review, during which a commitment must be made to start the next phase. Of course, those familiar with PRINCE2 will recognize this as the 'go/no go' decision point.

A description of the main phases of the spiral model follows, and Figure 4 illustrates the model in graphical form.

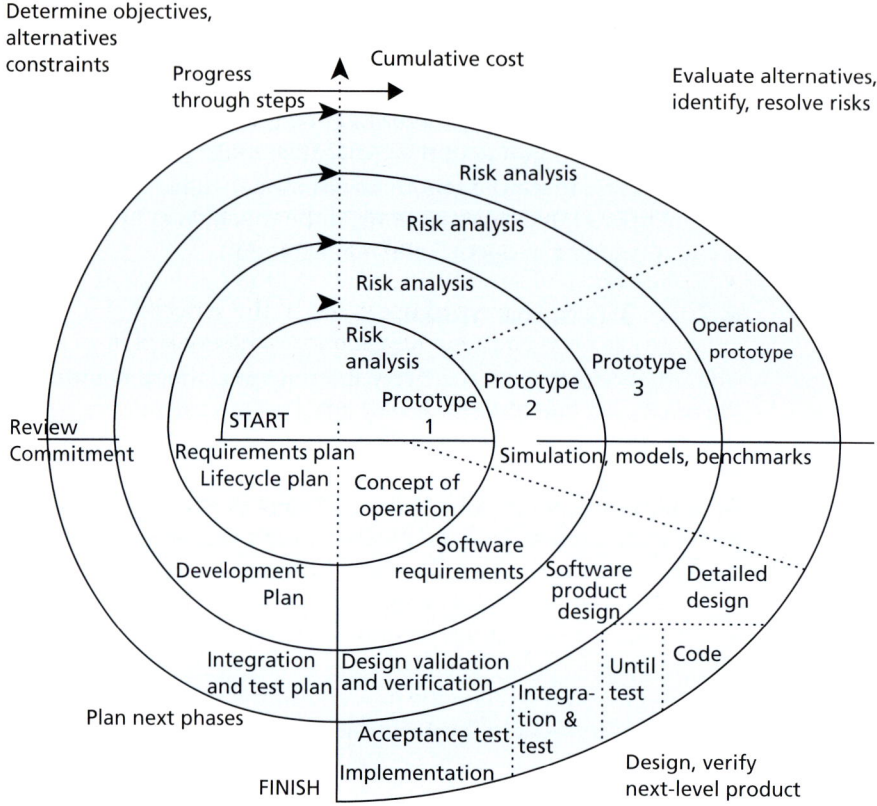

Figure 4: The Spiral Model (Boehm)

Phase 1 - Concept of Operation:

- Initiation
  - business request for a new IT service; determine objectives, alternatives and constraints at this phase
- Risk
  - perform risk analysis, possibly prototyping some of the ideas; evaluate alternatives and resolve risks
- Development Planning
  - define the concept of operation of the service
  - generate a requirements plan and a lifecycle plan

Phase 2 - Requirements Definition:

- Initiation
  - examine the requirements plan and determine objectives, alternatives and constraints at this phase
- Risk
  - perform risk analysis, possibly prototyping some of the ideas, evaluate alternatives and resolve risks
- Development Planning
  - software requirements analysis and definition
  - generate a development plan

Phase 3 - Product Design:

- Initiation
  - examine the development plan and determine objectives, alternatives and constraints at this phase
- Risk
  - perform risk analysis, producing an operational prototype to help evaluate alternatives and resolve risks
- Development Planning
  - software product design, and design validation and verification
  - generate integration and test plan

Phase 4 - Detailed design, coding, testing, integration, acceptance and implementation:

- Initiation
  - examine the design, and the integration and test plans, and determine objectives, alternatives and constraints
- Risk
  - perform risk analysis, possibly prototyping some of the ideas, evaluate alternatives and resolve risks

- Development Planning
  - detailed design, coding, unit test, integration and test, acceptance test and implementation
- Plan for next phases

Keep in mind the two key activities of the spiral model that are featured in each phase:

- re-consideration of objectives, alternatives, and constraints before the main work of the phase starts
- risk analysis, prototyping and the use of simulations and models to help evaluate alternatives and contain risks

The first three phases of the spiral model are each concerned with identifying the concept of operational requirements and design of an IT service or system. The fourth phase contains all of the conventional development stages from detailed design through to implementation. This model places great emphasis on the early stages of development, so that uncertainties about requirements and design can be identified and resolved before commitment to final development and implementation. Once more, the involvement of operations personnel focuses on the service delivery managers.

The value of the model is obvious when it is applied to IT designs where the requirements are volatile. The risk analysis and prototyping activities allow an organization to understand the full implications of the IT service they are proposing. From the IT developer's point of view, it enables a set of requirements to be generated where the major issues have been identified and resolved. From the operations angle, costs (and charges) can at least be estimated, and capacity and availability issues, considered. It is also possible to consider service levels and the impact on continuity/contingency plans, but the impact on service support is still limited. The configuration management process (a struggle for most organizations) is the only process that can realistically be considered.

The spiral model enables customers and operational managers to specify their own requirements to the development teams once risks and uncertainties have been resolved in the earlier phases. However, the model, like others, lacks a definition of the *maintenance* stage.

4.2.4 Agile and Rapid Prototyping Models

These lifecycles also are mostly variants of the spiral model.

Agile methods:
Agile methods are largely an answer to requests from the business for *lighter* methods to create a faster, slicker software development process,

in particular with regard to development for the internet and mobile technology services. Some of the more common methods will be outlined, in addition to some of the most obvious flaws and benefits.

Very little is known about the investment benefit of agile methods (or evolutionary methods) and there has been little real research into the 'best' method to use. As a result, all of them can be considered a risk to both development and operations. Also, there are no (current) procedures available for selection of the method, making it even more difficult for operations to fully understand and integrate with service development.

The agile movement documented a 'manifesto' in 2001 (Beck *et al*, Cockburn) with four central values:

- individuals and interactions over processes and tools
- working software over comprehensive documentation
- customer collaboration over contract negotiation
- responding to change over following a plan

Even cursory knowledge of *any* of the versions of ITIL will cause alarm bells to ring with many readers of this 'manifesto'. The values, if not contradictory to ITIL are, at best, orthogonal to it.

ITIL practitioners will recognize an immediate issue with attempting to design services from the operations standpoint. The issues are with the importance of process being diminished, the possible high frequency of code change, contracts becoming less important and change management becoming a burden.

It follows then, that knowledge of the methods used, will be imperative to any successful collaboration.

Figure 5 (Boehm; 2002) shows the spectrum of planning, now in the sight lines of operations. Note also that CMM (Capability Maturity Model) is not operable in the agile arena without considerable effort; it covers more structured domains.

Researchers such as Hawrysh and Ruprecht (2000) have stated that a single method cannot work across the entire spectrum, and that project management should identify the specific nature of projects and select the best development method. Logically, this should extend to planning for inclusion of IT Service Management practitioners. Many research papers on what is often called 'plan driven methodologies', do not even include the classic IT Service Management processes as reference points.

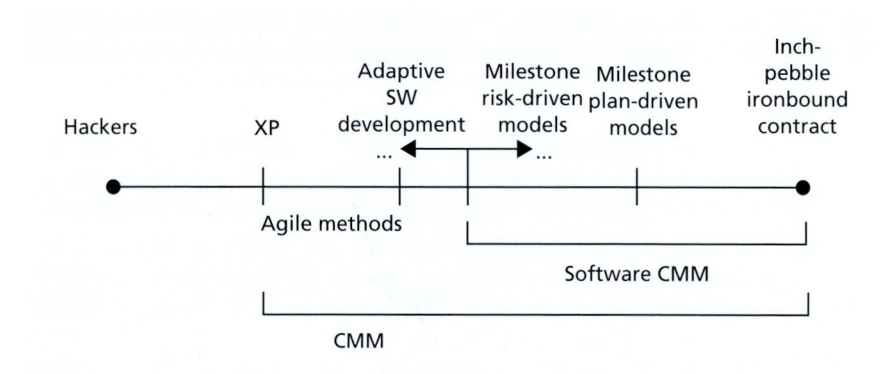

```
                                              Inch-
                      Adaptive  Milestone Milestone   pebble
                         SW    risk-driven plan-driven ironbound
    Hackers    XP    development  models    models    contract
                         ...◄──────────►...
    ●──────────┼─────────┼─────────┼─────────┼─────────●
                    Agile methods   |                         |
                                    |    Software CMM         |
                |                                     |
                          CMM
```

Figure 5: The Planning Spectrum (Boehm)

Agile Methods

Dynamic Systems Development Method (DSDM)

In the UK at least, DSDM is the one of the most important of the Rapid Application Development (RAD) methods. DSDM is not-for-profit and non proprietary, and is maintained by the DSDM Consortium. There are parallels with ITIL, but DSDM is much more open and has a framework of controls for RAD, complemented by guidance on efficient use of the controls.

The approach can be summarized in the following way; instead of attending to the degree of functionality in a product and then adjusting time/resources to reach the goals, time/resource issues are addressed **first** and the functionality addressed after that point.

There are five phases to DSDM: feasibility study, business study, functional model iteration, design and build iteration and implementation. Clearly, the first two phases are performed only once. Figure 6 provides an overview of DSDM.

The suitability of DSDM is considered in the feasibility study. Operations managers are advised to become deeply involved during both this phase and in the business study phase, to ensure their input is made in good time.

In total, DSDM defines fifteen roles, none of them taking cognizance of ITIL roles. It is recommended that operations personnel seek to be nominated at least as 'adviser user', which is an additional, but recognized role, in order to be able to provide input as appropriate.

As with all RAD methods, change is the norm, which means ITIL ideology will be challenged to deal with change therein described as best practice.

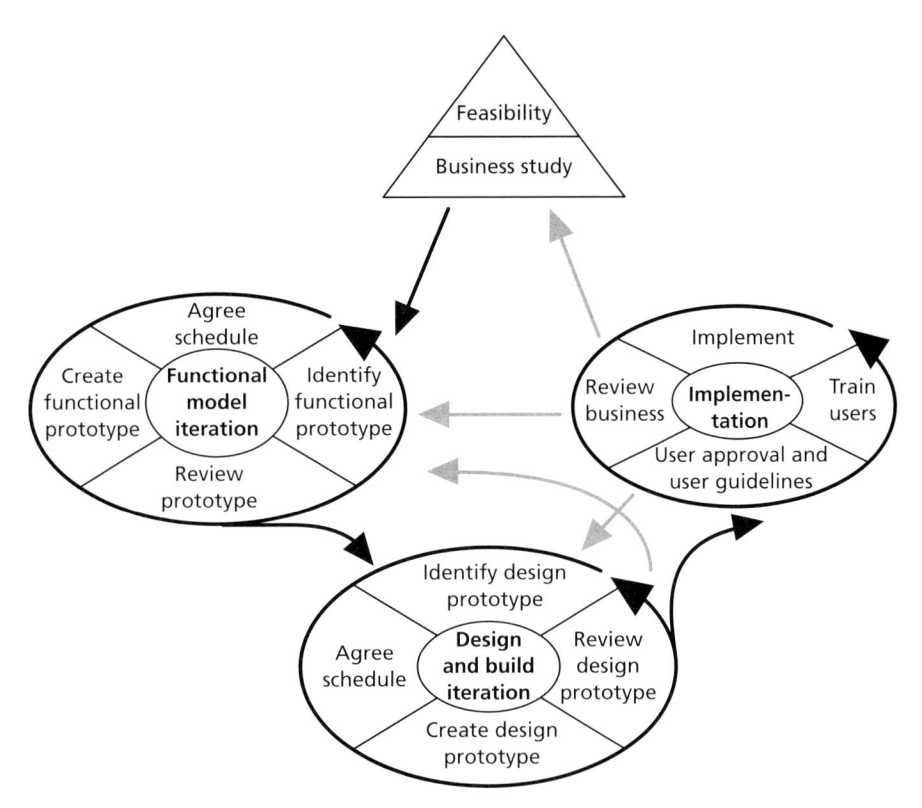

Figure 6: DSDM Process Model (Stapleton)

It will be necessary to fully comprehend how change will come about and be responsive (and adaptable) to the nature of the development. Failure to embrace the method and to attempt to impose ITIL framework, will simply cause strife.

Note: In 2002, an eDSDM version of the method was released focusing on eBusiness and eCommerce.

Scrum (System Configuration Recover Utilization and Methodology)
Scrum was developed to manage the systems development process. It is evidence based, applying ideas from industrial process control theory to development. It does not define particular development techniques; instead, Scrum concentrates on how a team would function flexibly in a changing environment.

The principal concept is that requirements, time frames, resources and technology are variables that must be managed, not unlike PRINCE2, and it involves frequent management activities aimed at continuous improvement of the development process. CMM proponents will recognize similarities too. Scrum is considered to form a project management framework for other methods, such as Extreme Programming (XP).

Extreme Programming (XP)

XP evolved from the problems of long development cycles. It covers five phases: exploration, planning, iteration to release, production-ready maintenance and death.

The exploration phase, where customers write 'story cards' describing service features, is the most obvious touch point for operations. Each phase will require different (though mainly service delivery) skills, and an understanding of the method needs to be in place if proper interaction is to be achieved.

Documentation does not take place until the 'death' phase; an interesting approach for those of who grew up with maintaining undocumented systems.

Feature Driven Development (FDD)

Principally, FDD focuses on design and building of a system or service. It claims to be suitable for building critical systems and services (unlike most of the others). Figure 7, provides a simplified diagram.

The emphasis is on the quality of design and, in essence, it is an iterative method of development. Planning by feature includes development of a high level plan. Clearly, co-ordinating the build of each 'feature' and their cumulative effects on IT operations would be the key.

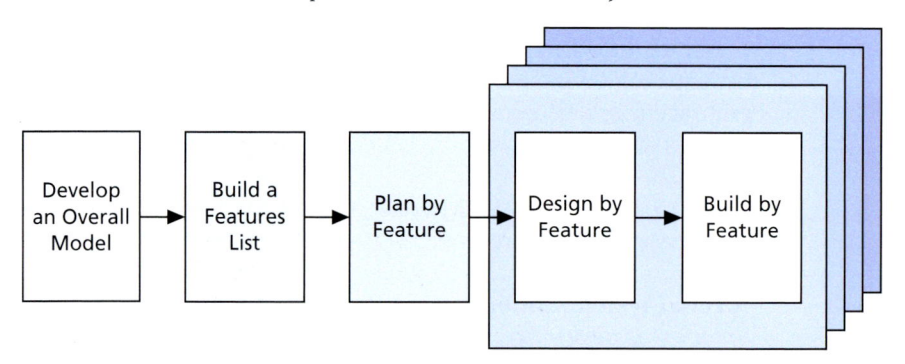

Figure 7: Processes of Feature Driven Development

Crystal Family

The emphasis is on iteration, communication and co-operation. Crystal is, essentially, a family of methods, color-coded to allow proper selection of the most appropriate technique. The coding is based on project size and criticality, and assumes that more rigor is required for critical projects than for others.

Rational Unified Process (RUP)

RUP is also a highly iterative method; this time mainly for object oriented systems development. It comprises four phases: inception, elaboration, construction and transition, each of which is split into iterations. Inception is where the objectives of the lifecycle are stated (and is, therefore, a key stage for ITIL processes to be established). Project planning is part of elaboration, and also includes detailed descriptions of the process, infrastructure and development environment. Because RUP emphasizes automation, support for automation is also described in this phase.

Transition is considered to be a phase in which subsequent releases are made to correct problems or complete postponed features, both of which may be of interest to the change management functions.

Throughout each phase, nine workflows take place in parallel. The influence of the spiral model can be seen here: business modeling, requirements, analysis and design, implementation, test, configuration and change management, project management and environment. Most are self evident, and it is equally clear that ITIL processes can be integrated once a proper understanding of RUP is achieved.

Adaptive Software Development (ASD)

ASD focuses on the issues in development of more complex, larger services. It has been described as 'balancing on the edge of chaos', once again not exactly a description designed to inspire those working within a process culture. The phases are described as speculate, collaborate and learn, and they are named to emphasize the role of change in a process. A relatively inexact definition of the end product is created and it is accepted that change is inevitable. ASD is focused on the result of the process and the quality, rather than tasks or processes, used to produce it.

Other types of RAD Methods

Organizations may select elements of the spiral model to develop their own evolutionary and prototyping lifecycle models. The way in which these lifecycles are executed may vary considerably from one organization to another according to the technologies available. Some methods, notably SSADM, include requirements prototyping as an intrinsic core and provide separate guidance on the use of other types of prototyping.

IT services developed in this way *may* be directly transferable into production environments. Of course, this approach disallows any interaction from IT operations in terms of planning for impact and (except for urgent developments) should, on grounds of security and compliance, be discouraged.

The initial aims of these models should not be overextended; eg the purpose of a prototyping environment may be simply to generate a functioning service which the customer can assess, and no more. If an IT service produced in this way is placed into production, then many operational management requirements may well have been ignored. And as indicated above, it is almost certain that insufficient attention has been paid to governance, security and compliance issues, let alone the quality of the design.

If, however, the aim is to produce a production system, then there must be clear boundaries to show at which time prototyping and operational management become involved in the development stages (and indeed, where prototyping is to be stopped).

In terms of planning and implementing a lifecycle, the use of these models raises a number of issues. A key question is where and how operational managers should be involved with projects based on these models?

The purpose of prototyping may be to demonstrate functions to a customer quickly, so that requirements can be refined. As a result, a decision may be taken that operational management concerns are not relevant at this time. However, once the requirements have been agreed, thought then needs to be given as to where and how the operational management functions are integrated with the development of a production system. Note again that the issue is the domain specificity; the roles of development and operations are very different and the key to success is finding a champion at a sufficiently influential level to bring the two functions together and encourage a co-operative environment. It is likely that traditional IT Service Management practitioners will move towards a greater understanding of the wider business drivers and to ways of working with colleagues to achieve them.

For projects using an iterative, or agile solution, the situation is different. During one cycle of the model, the stages are explicit and lead directly to a production system. Therefore the involvement of operational managers can be planned and implemented in a similar way to the waterfall model. However, the production system is not completed in one cycle and further cycles are required. This has consequences for implementing the co-operative procedures described in this book.

The problem is that the total operational management support required for the completed service, cannot be determined until all of the evolutionary iterations have been executed.

For example, during one cycle capacity management may be able successfully to plan and meet the capacity needs for the production system delivered at the end of that cycle. However, as more cycles are executed, so capacity needs will accumulate to cope with the expanding system. Only when all of the cycles are complete can the total capacity requirements be assessed, and by that time they may have become unacceptable.

4.2.5 Issues

None of the agile methods make it easy for operational management to align appropriate process interfaces. In every case, a broad understanding of the model in use is needed, and a Service Design Activity Matrix (SDAM see Chapter Eight) should be created from scratch on every occasion that development and operations are in discussion.

DSDM differs from other methods with its use of prototyping, and roles such as 'ambassador' and 'adviser', that allow operations the opportunity both to understand the conceptual framework more easily, and to identify appropriate interfaces. The drawback is the requirement to belong to the DSDM Consortium in order to gain access to white papers that provide insight; this is seen as a hurdle to acceptance, and one of which others should be aware.

When the operational management functions are being introduced during a project using an agile model, additional activities may be required between cycles to assess the growing demands on the IT infrastructure, and to predict the final level of support required.

4.2.6 Summary

The lifecycle model is a principal tool of the project manager. It acts as input to resource and timescale planning and as a means of navigation during the project. It can also be a tool for a manager procuring a development system: in order to ensure quality in a system that is being procured, a procurer will often require that a defined, approved process is used by the developer. This is one way in which a quality management system (QMS), certified to ISO 9001, can assist procurement. By nominating a lifecycle model at the outset, the developer can demonstrate that they have a well founded strategy for development. During the project, the procurer can check that the developer is conforming to the stated model, or justify any deviation from the model.

It is also important to note that a method is not a lifecycle model. A method defines how activities should be carried out, and might place constraints on the lifecycle in some way; for instance, SSADM prescribes that certain products be developed in a certain order, and to that extent, constrains the lifecycle model within which it is used. Experienced practitioners of SSADM apply common sense when using the default process model, in order to minimize the extent of any constraint.

There are underlying concerns about the use of lifecycle models if they have an overtly prescriptive approach. Some lifecycle models, such as the spiral model, simply seem to ignore the fact that service requirements cannot be stated fully in advance, and that the development process itself actually influences the final outcome.

CHAPTER 5 Assessment and Selection of Lifecycle Models

5.1 Introduction

This chapter provides guidance on the assessment and selection of an appropriate lifecycle model for an IT service design. The selection of a model is NOT the responsibility of operations, and this chapter is written only to provide an overview of the issues that are involved in the selection process.

It is not assumed that readers are familiar with the finer details of the most commonly used models (see Chapter Four for further background on these models); for IT service design personnel, one would imagine that, unless they once had a career in development, this is unlikely. Again, this illustrates the core of the dilemma of the service design approach, and draws attention to the people skills that will be needed to engage sceptical managers who are working in another IT domain.

The first task is to identify the key requirements of the proposed service. There are many requirements which influence the decision as to which lifecycle model to use. However, within many organizations, standard models, along with method descriptions and supporting toolsets, may be preferred. In this case, the task of model selection is that of adapting an existing model for a new service, rather than a free choice. It will not be the service designer who can make the choice and it will be up to that individual (and their team) to educate the operations side about choice and use of any model, and interactions needed. As should be clear by now, service delivery functions are much more important to planning, and a sea change in current organizational maturity will almost certainly be needed, thereby throwing many ITIL adoption plans into disarray. Current projects to improve or adopt service support processes will allow useful interaction at the testing and pre-production phases, but little else.

The following three sections give guidance on how to perform assessment and selection in either of these situations.

5.2 Attributes

There are several attributes which affect the decision to use a particular lifecycle model. They include:

- service type (eg batch, on-line, interactive, real-time, function strong or data centric)
- the degree of uncertainty about the functions; for example, the ability to specify the requirements interfaces with other services (ie is there sharing of lifecycles?)
- expected annual Change traffic (eg the degree of change in response to new business needs timeframes for development); where critical schedules are involved, different models may imply different risks of meeting the service or system size (ie the general size and complexity of a service or system may require tailoring a model)

5.2.1 Service type

In this context, service type means one that is either data oriented or function oriented. The differences between these types of IT service in terms of lifecycle model selection are substantial.

Data oriented services are most commonly found in commercial organizations. They reflect business processes in which there are defined sets of information upon which certain transactions operate. A service like this could be built using a structured method such as SSADM. By contrast, a function oriented service is one where the base data structures may be manipulated by many types of processes. An example of this is a CGI system, where structured methods are almost certainly unsuitable.

Commercial or business services are generally driven by business rules which state the data that is required and how the data is to be processed. In this way requirement definitions and service specifications can be more easily determined with a model that uses a top-down approach.

In such cases it is rarely possible to produce final requirement definitions and specifications in a single pass through the stages.

5.2.2 Uncertainty of requirements

Another attribute, which is very closely related to the previous one, is whether a service can be specified with sufficient accuracy to allow a document or data driven model (eg waterfall) to be used, or whether another model is required to account for greater risks of change during development. Here again, there is a likely source of conflict; the ITIL change management processes do not transfer easily to development processes. Changing code in development is not the same as changing something for release to production.

A service may be defined as a data centric, transaction oriented system, which initially suggests that the waterfall model may be appropriate. However, if the business function being considered is new and immature, eg to support a new product, then the requirements and specifications of this function may not be clear. An organization may have to consider moving away from waterfall-based models to spiral-based models. However, irrespective of this, the operations side will continue to need to invest in improving service delivery functions, even at the expense in the short term of service support processes.

Projects to improve IT are not always well-funded, and for those organizations who are short of investment money, tough decisions will be needed on what to spend on. The organizational changes required to invest in the guidance of ITIL should never be underestimated; consider also at this juncture, the investment in training related to version 2 and version 3. Unless version 3 training providers are expert in systems analysis and design (and their trainers can prove this), as well as lifecycle modeling and ITIL, you may well ponder on the value of the training and its outcome.

5.2.3   Interfaces with other services

The IT service, and its interfaces with other services, may also determine the lifecycle model chosen. This is particularly true for organizations using Information Engineering techniques to generate corporate process and data models, and also where there is some standardization of lifecycle models. In these cases, lifecycle models usually have to work within the constraints of the methods, techniques and tools used to execute them. Even if a sequential waterfall model is used, there is still the need in any given service/systems development to assess its suitability, and determine if extra stages are required to cope with unknowns and risks.

5.2.4   Annual Change traffic

The expected degree of change (or annual change traffic) during operation of a service can have a significant effect upon lifecycle model selection. Where it is known that the business area supported by the service is volatile, then the chosen model must be capable of handling a high rate of change. It must lead to a relatively open design, with appropriate documentation, which allows for significant changes to be made. This consideration is probably applicable to many commercial systems, especially those with high capital investment and a long anticipated life. In this respect, the objective of the development stages is not merely to produce an operational system, but also to produce one designed for change. The use of models to plan for maintenance is discussed in more detail later. This is a particular point of interest for those using ITIL, since this consideration is not highlighted. ITIL remains interpretative, and this area, one where technology will form a key facilitator, is not addressed, despite its clear impact on planning for service support processes and interactions, and, of course, scalability.

5.2.5 Timeframes for development

The schedule for development and implementation of a service may also have an impact on lifecycle selection. If it is necessary to generate some service functions in a very short period of time, then the model selected will need to enable rapid development, whilst at the same time identifying the risks being taken. As with ITIL, SSADM, or your choice of method, it is neither infallible nor intended to be used as a blunt instrument. Smart people will always allow for the constraints of methods and frameworks, and not simply use them as templates (really as substitutes for creativity) with inevitable consequences to acceptance and suitability.

5.2.6 Service size

Another attribute that affects lifecycle model selection is the estimated service size and complexity. The development of large and complex services may have to be subdivided into smaller projects, and the lifecycle model used may need to support consecutive and concurrent development. Essentially this will necessitate a high degree of program management skills to manage all of the projects. Also, more complex services may require additional activities to be specified within lifecycle stages. By comparison, it is rarely recommended to break down a small project into the same level of detail as a large one.

5.3 Assessment of Existing Models

One way to evaluate an existing model is to analyze its effects on the management of the operations, and the ability to deliver services which meet infrastructure needs. Each operational management function may contribute to this process. Some of the more prominent sources of information are:

- service level agreement reports
- service availability reports
- problem management reports
- capacity management analyses
- change traffic analysis
- productivity assessments
- cost management reports

If a service fails to meet the requirements specified for operations, an internal evaluation may be made. The purpose is to assess maintainability and how well lifecycle stages were implemented. A number of techniques may be used, including:

- design and code analysis measures
- documentation analysis
- methods and tools analysis
- quality audits

The best advice here is to use the organizational change suggested later for the IT service design team (or use internal IT auditors), as developers will not welcome IT operations leading an audit. From the external analysis, a view can be obtained of the effectiveness of the current lifecycle model to deliver services which meet service requirements. From the internal analysis, reasons can be found which explain why a service does not meet the requirements. By combining these analyses, assessments of a lifecycle model can be made in terms of its ability to:

- deliver services which conform to specifications
- deliver services to meet schedules
- deliver maintainable services
- provide an acceptable maintenance environment
- manage the maintenance process

5.3.1 Selection of a Lifecycle Model

The next stage of selection is to consider the attributes of the planned service against proposed models. This task is performed by addressing the following questions:

- Are all the necessary lifecycle processes defined?
- Are the processes subject to quality management?
- Are the processes subject to project management?
- Is the model suitable for the service type and size?
- Does the model offer the required degree of productivity?
- Are there acceptable methods and tools support for the model?
- Does the model cover the entire service life in an integrated way?
- Does the model address compliance, risk and security issues?
- Does the model allow all IT and business staff the right degree of involvement at different stages?
- Are skills and training available for the model?

With any IT development project, particularly in rapidly changing business environments, it is strongly recommended that current lifecycle models are reassessed and modified where appropriate, and not simply adopted for historical reasons. If service design is to have a real impact instead of being fashionable, it must be influential in this area.

5.3.2 Modification of a lifecycle model

After a lifecycle model has been selected, consideration needs to be made as to the detailed application of a given service or development project. This tailoring process is essential to ensure that only the relevant activities and tasks defined by a model are implemented. It is widely accepted that one of the main reasons for past failures in the use of models is a lack of thought given to their use.

What lifecycle diagrams *cannot* show is the number and potential complexity of the many tasks and activities which may take place within each lifecycle stage. An organization needs to have developed detailed descriptions before any tailoring can begin.

While the modification process is primarily the responsibility of the development and maintenance staff, the IT services designer will need to ensure that the effects of any modifications are reviewed by appropriate operational managers. At this stage it is worth highlighting again what, for many, may be obvious; the service designer needs to be capable in both the development **and** operations fields, or to have staff drawn from experience of both.

CHAPTER 6 Interfaces with Major Management and Planning Activities

6.1 Introduction

Figure 8 illustrates the major planning activities of software developers, maintainers and operational management. It shows the levels of planning for information systems, starting with the business strategy. The illustration maps out the *business* view of their demand for IT.

Program management can be viewed as the integration of a series of disparate work projects which, when managed as a coherent body of work, provide benefits to the organization which would not be realized if those projects were managed separately. Operational planning (or IT planning) may be the result of examining the IT requirements of each of the work programs; it is true, however, that operational planning may, in some instances be, in itself, a program of work.

At the highest levels, business and other strategies are studied, so that IS strategies and plans are designed to meet the requirements of the businesses.

At the next level, the demand for IT is turned into more detailed and realizable plans of action.

The programs of work identified in the business strategy are refined into programs of specific projects at the next level (program planning). Changes to the supporting operations may be managed and planned at this level (operational planning).

Individual projects and studies are shown at the lowest level, together with operational activities of planning and controlling the computers and networks of an organization, upon which applications systems and IT services are built and run.

The ITIL processes not only interact with other areas in the IT environment and the business, but within the IT infrastructure itself, as can be seen in Figure 9. In practice, there will be many such relationships and dependencies; the most important ones are discussed in this book.

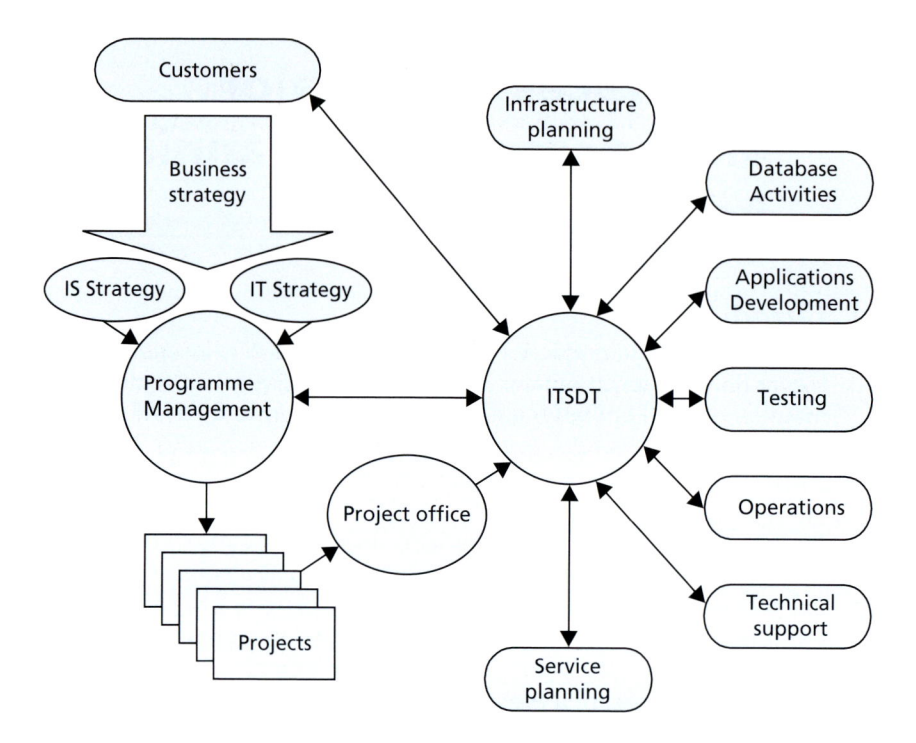

Figure 8: ITSDT in the Context of the Environment

6.2 Role of the IT Planning Unit

An IT Planning Unit or a Program Support Office would be ideally placed to co-ordinate the high level planning activities necessary to integrate program planning with software lifecycle support. It is recommended that a Program Board is assigned the responsibility for design authority, including selection and allocation of appropriate lifecycles (in consultation with software developers).

Monitoring of the interactions between software development and operational management should be carried out by the Program Support Office, the IT Planning Unit (or the Project Support Office, if there is no IT Planning Unit) and the IT service design team. It is vital that planning and monitoring activities are properly co-ordinated, so that planning and lifecycle selection can be closely aligned.

There must be effective communication between:

- IS planners and operational planners - plans for a new or revised IT infrastructure, which interface with plans for software development, may well be part of a program of work, and it is essential that the overall impact on the current IT infrastructure is assessed
- IS planners and IT planners in the IT Planning Unit - so that appropriate software lifecycle models can be selected for use in the resulting IS/IT Projects
- IT Planning Unit and software developers - to participate in selection of the appropriate software lifecycle models and to identify key milestones
- IT Planning Unit and operational planners - to agree appropriate milestones and the interfaces between lifecycle support models and operational plans
- Operational managers and software developers - to identify in detail the key interfaces and how best to co-ordinate software lifecycle support activities; the Service Design Activity Matrix (SDAM) is used for this purpose
- IT service designers and all domains - including any customer liaison functions that may exist

6.3 IT Service Design Team (ITSDT)

In a number of organizations, an ITSDT is drawn from people with business acumen, systems analysis and design skills and technical skills, and is created to manage the day-to-day interfaces between the business side, development, testing, technical services - such as database design and administration - and operations. The ITSDT works closely with whatever planning or project offices may exist, and its roles, depending on the size of the organization, are:

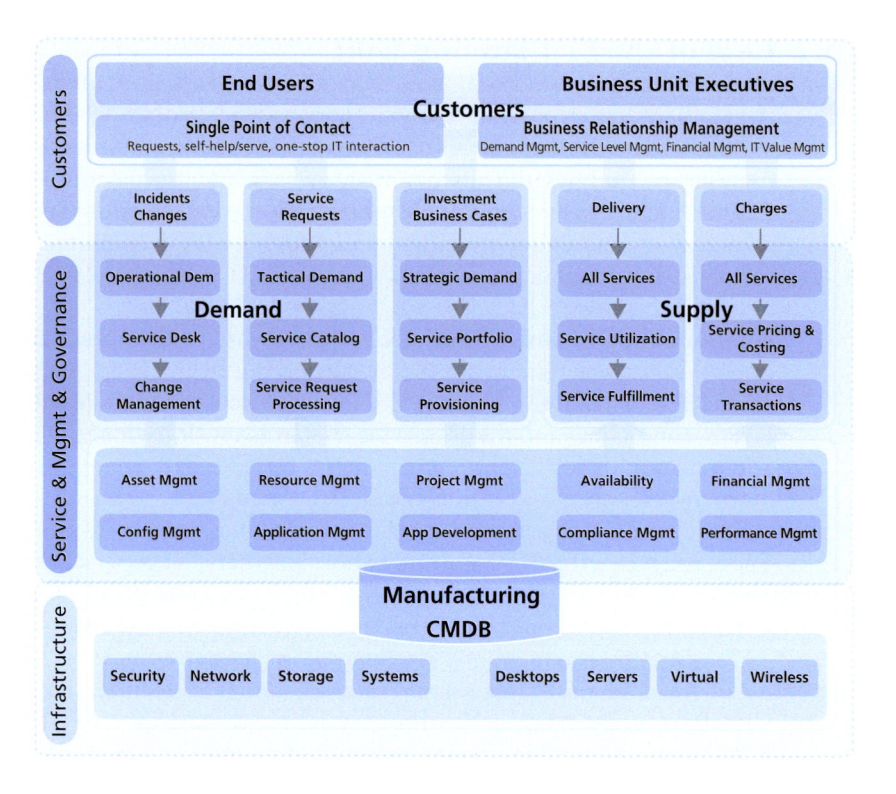

Figure 9: (expanded from Figure 2) The Relationships

- principal point of contact for the business in regards to availability of and problems with the operational service (in some organizations, major developments may be underway that cause numerous development/testing environments to be in place at any one time, allowing for major releases of applications throughout the management of a program)
- liaison between all technical domains
- post mortem analysis of all major outages
- co-ordination of all activities affecting live service, including chairing Change Advisory Boards as a wholly neutral body
- co-ordinating change management of services in development including scheduling testing and go-live activities
- reporting to all IT domains summaries of issues affecting the business
- co-ordinating activities around requests for change to live services and services in development
- reporting to the business about scheduled and unscheduled outages and impact
- creating high level schedules (HLS) of applications so that, for example, batch runs take place after online transactions have been input and dependencies between programs (to allow, for example, for coherent management reports) are run at the appropriate times

The ITSDT should not sit in either the development domain or the operational domain; to function effectively it must be independent of both. Nor does it take over the day-to-day activities of, for example, the change or business continuity roles. The team is generally (depending on the organization) relatively small, with two people co-ordinating live activities (an IT Service Co-ordinator (ITSC), with a less experienced deputy, who is able to fill-in when the ITSC is away), two more people assigned to 'next phase' development activities (Development Services Co-ordinators and deputies) - the number of phases will determine overall size - and some people assigned to administrative support.

The ITSDT will be led by a senior figure well versed in *all* domains, and each of the two person teams will feature one very experienced manager, ideally with experience of both development and operations.

Figure 10 illustrates how the live teams and development teams in the ITSDT maintain continued involvement with programs of work. Essentially the Development Co-ordinators replace the live service co-ordinators upon go-live of the project divisions of work that they have been managing, with the live service team taking on the roles of other sections of work scheduled for development.

For clarity, the diagram illustrates two development divisions.

By far the most important feature of the ITSDT role is that neither IT operations nor IT development is threatened by being subservient to

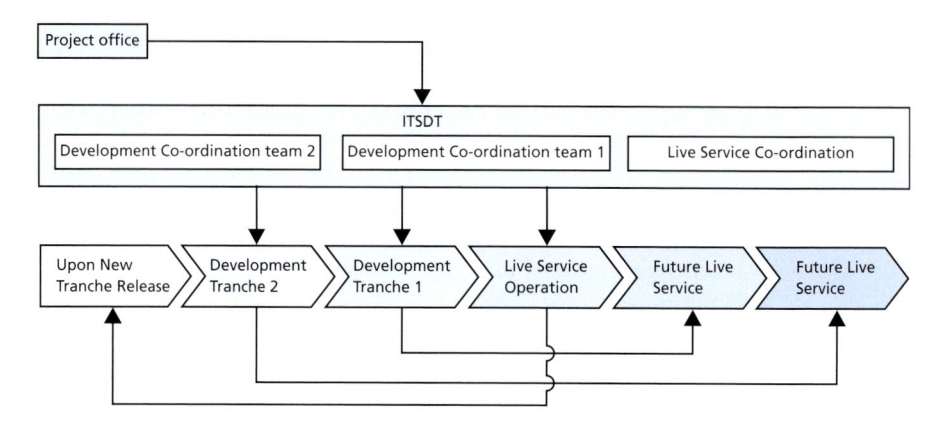

Figure 10: ITSDT and Project co-ordination

another domain. It is an unfortunate fact that such political manipulation is necessary because of the very different management issues, frameworks and models employed, and the aspirations of the two domains.

6.4 Using Lifecycle Models in the ITSDT

When the introduction of a new IT service is being considered or is ready to be built, installed and operated, the work should be planned so that activities take place in the most appropriate order, and in a way that minimizes risk and increases quality. The resulting logical plan for the project is the *lifecycle model*. The lifecycle model provides the structure within which the following, can be identified:

- what major activities have to be done (the HLS)
- what the dependencies are between them
- what major products or services the activities will create
- major milestones - that is, the point at which products will be delivered allowing plans to be drawn up with the Testing teams for integrated systems testing, customer tests and pre-go live testing

A lifecycle model is different from a project plan in one significant way. The lifecycle model can be interpreted in many different ways because it has decision points and iterations in it, and the outcome might not be finalized until the project is under way. A project plan is a single representation and is a management tool showing which activities will take place in which order; it will not be open-ended.

It follows that a rigorous plan cannot be drawn up before an appropriate model has been designed. The design of the lifecycle model depends on the security, compliance, risks and quality requirements specific to the development or post-development project in hand. Since every project will have its own particular set of risks and quality requirements, every software project will need its own lifecycle model to be designed for it. *There is, therefore, no single software lifecycle model that can be used for all projects.* It follows that the ITIL processes and roles involved will vary depending on the nature of the project. If, for example, an application suite is being designed for a bank, it will have different security and compliance requirements to that of a warehouse stock suite. It is true that some classes of development have similar requirements and some general lifecycles can be used as a starting point for lifecycle model design, though as with all things in IT, it is dangerous in terms of risk, to assume that generic models or frameworks are anything other than generic; and even more unsafe to act on opinion that is not supported by evidence.

6.5 Plans

Once a lifecycle model has been designed for a project, a plan can be drawn up. This involves looking at the decision points and iterations in the lifecycle, and either planning only as far as can be reasonably predicted or planning further by assuming the outcome of a decision or perhaps a limit on iteration. The resulting plan can then be resourced and scheduled in the traditional way for use in project control.

6.6 Relationship with Other IT Related Functions

Lifecycle support not only affects most operational management activities, but has a major effect on many other functions, some of which are outlined below. Relationships with operational management activities are described in more detail in Annex Three.

6.6.1 Quality Management

Quality software is specified and designed with quality in mind; although self-evident, this general rule is intended to demonstrate that it is not possible to fit the required quality and reliability at a later date. The cost of building in quality is more than offset by the saving (in cost and customer relations) in likely maintenance requirements that would result if quality requirements were ignored during development. Similarly, the availability of reliable software to customers of IT is, in turn, a benefit to the external businesses served by those customers. A small upfront investment will pay large dividends. More information is available in the ASL and CMM books.

Quality management activities should therefore take place throughout the lifecycle. They must be built into the design, selection and management of products and services, if the latter is to deliver the required performance.

6.6.2 Security Management

Security must also be considered throughout the lifecycle (as it should be with other operational management functions). This is particularly so during the software specification stage, as it is rarely possible to apply protective measures to an installed application retrospectively.

Security management should be considered:

- during the development process, eg in conjunction with any development method for determining the security features which need to be built into the software
- throughout the operational lifecycle of the service, at regular, predetermined intervals, to ensure continued protection whenever any alteration is made to the service, including software enhancements

6.6.3 Risk Management

Risk management is appropriate throughout because many types of risk (to the project, to the delivered product and to use of the product or service) need to be addressed at the outset. In essence, risks can be accepted, avoided, mitigated or managed. Generic risk descriptions offer only a guide and should, in fact, be classed as a risk to the project if they are accepted without criticism.

6.6.4 Compliance

And compliance, the industry buzzword of the 21st century, is an absolute pre-requisite, because retrofitting patches to fix compliance issues will not be acceptable to business or to legislators. As with measures taken within development to ensure deterrence of fraud, it will be common to specify applications that are compliant with legislation and capable of rigorous audit.

6.7 Cost/benefit Assessment

Adoption of the concepts of lifecycle support will provide the opportunity for organizations to identify at an early stage, areas for which costs and benefits must be documented. Cost/benefit assessment can be used throughout the lifecycle. It is used to:

- support the initial business case for software development, and show management 'what-if' options, such as maintaining a service in-house or by outsourcing

- check the success of the development phase in a post-implementation review to determine whether it is worthwhile to retrofit a new lifecycle to an existing service
- evaluate operational management options, such as the costs of porting a service to a new IT infrastructure
- provide on-going cost/benefit profile to show that an application is economically viable or that some remedial action is necessary to extend the useful economic life of a service (redevelopment is necessary)

The general steps in cost/benefit assessment are to:

- use the stages in the lifecycle model as the decision points for estimation of costs and success factors, and use a consistent method such as Function Point Analysis (FPA) or Constructive Cost Modeling (COCOMO) for sizing and estimating the costs of the development stages
- use the anticipated annual change traffic to estimate the maintenance costs during the expected services life, obtained from customer manager estimates of benefits which the proposed application will bring
- combine cost and benefit data in graphical models to show the cost/benefit profile over the anticipated life of the service

The initial cost/benefit information is maintained over the life of the service. It is updated:

- at the end of the development phase as part of the Project Evaluation Report (PER)
- at periodic intervals during maintenance, or if software starts to show symptoms of poor performance (ie the cost is too much in relation to what is being obtained from the software)

6.8 Organizational Issues

Implementing lifecycle support in IT may cause organizational change as teams move to new ways of working. The transition will need to be planned so that all staff are aware of their changed roles and responsibilities. The role of the IT Planning Unit, Program Support Office or Project Support Office and ITSDT are vital if the process of co-ordinating and integrating previously separate activities, is to be successful.

The guidance in this book is intended to help IT make a smooth transition to designing services and using lifecycles as tools. It should enable an organization to rapidly absorb change with the maximum beneficial effect.

CHAPTER 7 Planning for Service Design

7.1 Introduction

This section is intended to provide guidance on planning the introduction of lifecycle support as the means to service design. The main planning considerations fall under the following areas:

- appointment of an IT Service Co-ordinator (and the ITSDT)
- assessment and selection of lifecycle models
- using a lifecycle model to plan for operational management
- using a lifecycle model to plan for software maintenance
- application of lifecycle support to new and existing software services
- use of a Service Design Activity Matrix (SDAM)

Identification and documentation of the interfaces between a given lifecycle, customers of IT services and operational managers is a fairly complex and demanding task. There are many ITIL processes that may be active at various stages in the lifecycle. There are a variety of lifecycle models that may be chosen, each with its own effects on the IT infrastructure.

The approach adopted in this book is to describe generic planning procedures which can be tailored to the needs of individual projects. While the scope of the book does not include detailed descriptions of project management methods, again, it is recommended that PRINCE2 or PMI is adopted where appropriate.

7.1.1 Appoint an IT Service Co-ordinator

While the IT services manager retains the customary areas of responsibility, an IT Service Co-ordinator should be nominated, with the overall responsibility of ensuring that the individual operational managers are involved in all of the planning procedures described in the book.

There are various possible locations for this function within an organization. The function could be part of the Program Support Office, IT Planning Unit or Project Support Office, although some organizations may prefer to place it elsewhere within the IT environment as described earlier (such as the ITSDT), ensuring that it is perceived as independent of bias.

Figure 8 illustrated an example of a planning hierarchy, which shows that the IT service co-ordination takes place at the infrastructure planning level. It is likely that lifecycle support will have ramifications at all of the levels illustrated.

In addition to the overall goals described for the ITSDT, the terms of reference for the IT Service Co-ordinator should include:

- liaising with development and maintenance managers to identify planning requirements
- liaising with IT service managers to ensure that they are aware of their involvement and responsibilities in specific project plans
- participation in the selection and application of lifecycle models for operational planning
- appreciation of the benefits of using lifecycle models to plan for development and maintenance
- preparing plans for the IT infrastructure required to support individual IT services
- monitoring the implementation of the plans reporting progress to senior management and program managers
- performing Project Evaluation Reports (PERs), Post-Implementation Reviews (PIRs) and internal audits
- undertaking education and training of management and staff about the aims and objectives of lifecycle support

An initial plan for involving operational management in lifecycle support should be developed by the IT Service Co-ordinator, together with the Development Co-ordinator, with the key aim of describing the effectiveness and benefits of co-operation between software developers and operational managers. It is recommended that the plan centers initially on a pilot project based upon the procedures described here.

The plan should include the following steps:

- running awareness seminars and briefing staff on the aims and objectives of co-ordination
- illustrating interactions with IS/IT program planning and the benefits to be accrued from using the concepts
- selection of a project or system for the pilot, noting that the pilot should be kept small, and may apply either to a new development or to an existing system development of the implementation plan for the pilot
- using the planning procedures described here
- conducting a Project Evaluation Report of the pilot to determine how well it met the objectives

Following the pilot project, decisions can then be made as to the more general introduction of co-ordinated lifecycle support, and the scope of the plans can be widened to include more services.

7.1.2 Assessment and Selection of Lifecycle Models

The example application lifecycle, illustrated in Figure 11, covers development and use (production and maintenance) of an IT service. SSADM is used in the example only because it is a method that is known to the authors and that has the genealogy of development with two other OGC methods, PRINCE2 and, of course, ITIL.

It shows where SSADM activities fit into a full lifecycle, from initial planning to eventual decommissioning. SSADM is used for the development stages up to physical design and may also be used for maintenance (see the SSADM reference manuals for further details). Of course the stages of any structured method can be used.

It cannot be over stated that a lifecycle model is a *management* tool which provides a framework encompassing the elements of the software development and maintenance processes. It incorporates the procedures, controls and milestones from initial design through development, to installation and maintenance, and provides the milestones which enable progress to be assessed. Selection and use of the appropriate lifecycle model or models is not the responsibility of the operational managers. Their responsibility lies in defining (with the help of the ITSDT) the attributes and dependencies of a service to the business.

The Program Support Office, in consultation with software developers and the ITSC will be responsible for this task. It is essential, however, that operational managers are aware of the selection processes and of the impact on the IT infrastructure of using a particular lifecycle model.

7.1.3 Core Issues

The core issues in the selection process which should be addressed include:

1. What lifecycle models are available?
2. How well do existing models reflect business requirements?
3. Is some modification of the models currently used required?
4. Is more than one model necessary either for an individual service, or across a range of services?

It should not be assumed that a particular lifecycle model will meet the requirements of *all* services within an organization.

7.1.4 Major Considerations

Major considerations in the selection of a lifecycle model:

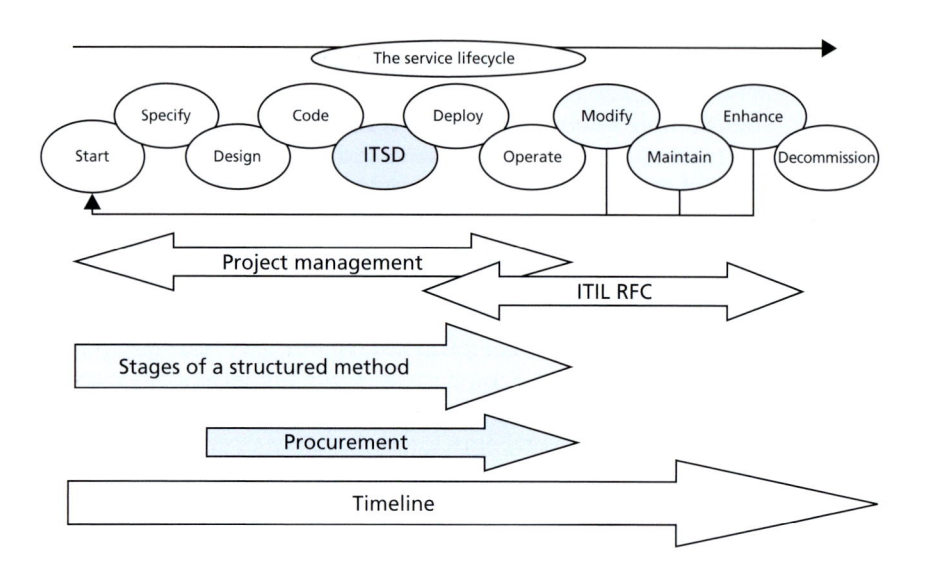

Figure 11: Project Portfolio Management and IT: The Service Lifecycle

- The model must be appropriate for the *type* of service (eg whether data or function centric, transaction based or interactive, whether functional or object oriented decomposition is required).
- It should be conformant with IS strategy and policy.
- The model must be documented and agreed upon, so that both quality and project management criteria are supported.
- It should define the maintenance stages clearly and in detail.
- It should enable metrics to be generated for assessing key factors such as productivity and quality.
- It should enable cost/benefit assessment of the operational management needed to support a new service using the developed software. The characteristics of services which affect lifecycle model selection should be identified, giving full weight to criteria which have the greatest importance in the maintenance stages.
- There should be some consideration of assessing any existing lifecycle models used within an organization, with the focus on the way such models affect the operational management and the delivery of an operational service.
- The treatment of modifications to a lifecycle model should be established, agreed and documented.

While it may well be the developers who may make the final recommendation of a lifecycle model, the IT Service Co-ordinator *must* participate in the assessment and selection process. This will ensure that the model provides the necessary features for the planning, organization, implementation and monitoring of operational management functions, all of which are fundamental if program planning is to be successful.

The selection of a lifecycle model may be performed as part of a feasibility study. The criteria should include a consideration of the basic question *'Do we have the IT infrastructure to develop and maintain a service of the type proposed?'* The answer will form part of the business case for the commissioning of a new development project.

CHAPTER 8 Using a Lifecycle Model to Plan for Operational Management Intervention

The purpose of this section is to outline the level of operational management planning required once a lifecycle model has been selected. A project management method such as PMI or PRINCE2 will provide the means to describe an overview of interactions (process), but an SDAM will be needed to provide detail (procedures for execution of processes). In general, some operational management functions are required throughout a lifecycle, while some may only be required during development, operations or maintenance. Also, as one progresses through the lifecycle, the importance of a particular operational management function is likely to change.

8.1 Identification and Management of Interfaces

There are many possible interactions between customers, developers, maintainers and the operational management teams, and these interfaces will depend upon the particular lifecycle model chosen and any modifications made to it. The first step is the identification and management of operational management interactions. In order to be effective the following planning steps are recommended:

- determine who is going to perform the tasks, and allocate resources
- identify how the operational managers will interface within the project environment, and determine the organization required
- develop an operational management support plan which shows the activity network, schedules, staffing, costs, timing and dependencies
- identify and document where and when specific operational management functions are active during the lifecycle
- document the tasks and deliverables required from each active operational management function at each lifecycle stage
- establish the size of the tasks, and estimate the resources needed and costs incurred to perform them
- determine when the tasks have to be performed, their dependencies on other tasks, and schedule them

8.2 Extensions to Models

The SDAM provided later in this chapter gives advice on how to document operational management activity within a lifecycle model. The key point is that any model requires refinement/extension so that the following interactions are understood for all stages of the lifecycle:

- at which lifecycle stages the different operational management functions are active for a given project
- the detail of operational management activity in terms of individual tasks, deliverables and resources involved

The same level of detail is required to describe the operational management activity for all environments. This will enable a consistent approach to be taken to project and quality management.

Quality management systems (QMS) procedures should be implemented at appropriate stages of the lifecycle. Building in quality - as with compliance and security - is the most cost-effective means of ensuring success.

Retrofitting of compliance, quality and security policies is not recommended. This is one reason to intervene at appropriate times; if compliance, quality and security are not able to be built in (for whatever reason - failure to implement an IT service design approach or the inability to interpret necessary inputs), the benefits of the approach will be negated and it is unlikely that the cost can be justified.

8.3 Generic Models

For organizations using a single lifecycle model, planning needs to be done only once in order to produce a generic lifecycle dependency plan for the organization. Thereafter, it can be modified for individual projects. As with all things 'general' it is important to have checks in place to ensure that the model is only used in situations for which it has been designed.

In many cases the role of an operational management function may change considerably as a service or product moves through the lifecycle. At the earlier stages, operational managers are involved with setting requirements and planning for the needs of the service in production. This requires organizations with a process culture, either to get up to speed rapidly with service delivery functions, or to place any project focused on IT service design on the back burner; this decision will be linked to costs and, no doubt, the ability of the organization to absorb the changes. During testing, the operational managers are concerned with validating that a service will meet these requirements (principally, the service support processes). During operational lifecycle management, managers will be concerned with managing service levels and responding to changing requirements; once again, this is largely service support.

Generic models for interaction are of interest, but they cannot be taken as the final word on what needs to be done; in Annex Three, this book describes some of the issues relating to specific processes. The purpose of the annex is to give an introduction to the major operational management functions, and indicate the type of interaction that needs to be initiated with developers and maintainers.

8.4 Using a Lifecycle Model to Plan for Software Maintenance

Operational management and software maintenance are very closely related. Historically, many organizations have failed to use models for maintenance, instead using them only to plan the development of services. This has led to a number of problems:

- Services have been developed which are either costly, or a challenge to maintain (or both).
- IT managers have to cope with operational problems caused by the lack of maintainability.
- The maintenance process has been poorly designed, understood and implemented, which has meant that the operational managers have not been able to play their part.

8.4.1 Operational Management and Software Maintainability

Two activities should be considered:

- the involvement of operational management in the development stages of each project, to ensure that maintainable services are designed (getting the product right in relation to maintainability)
- planning and implementing how operational managers and the maintainers will interact during the operational life of a service (defining the maintenance process correctly)

In the context of service design and lifecycle support, maintainability is defined as the ease with which a software system or service can be adapted when errors or deficiencies are identified. To assess the relationship between operational management and software maintainability, two questions need to be answered:

1. How does software maintainability impact operations management?
2. How can software maintainability be managed to include operational requirements?

Software maintainability, or the lack of it, may affect operational management in many ways. Some examples are:

- unstable software will become expensive to maintain over time, leading to an increase in incidents, and increased workloads on operational management disciplines such as Service Desk, service level management, computer operations, availability and problem management
- with software that is difficult to change, the time taken to repair production failures will become unacceptable (assuming the application is business critical), leading to degraded service levels
- software with degraded maintainability may become increasingly difficult to test, leading to excessive costs and resources needed for operational testing

These issues lead to poor agility in responding to change, and the inability to leverage existing software investment (software re-use). Software maintainability is a quality issue. That is, maintainability requirements need to be specified, implemented and validated during the development stages, under the control of a quality management system. Some requirements will be determined by maintainers, some by operations management staff, and some may be common to both.

8.4.2 Operational Management and the Maintenance Process

This section is concerned with interaction between operational management functions and the maintenance process.

The recommended approach is to use change management procedures to document the maintenance of software. The stages of specifying, designing and implementing a change are mapped as far as possible to the change management process. Note that this does not impact the development process, only the maintenance process. The stages should be described in the same way as for development. This approach not only promotes the concept of maintenance and maintainability as part of continued development, but also enables the continued involvement of operations management during maintenance.

The aim is to extend the use of lifecycle models. Too often, maintenance has been shown as a single process which follows the development stages and is not extended throughout the lifecycle. This lack of understanding and definition has led to the problems described earlier. Two key questions are raised:

1. What are the component parts of the maintenance process?
2. How should operational managers, in particular those working in live operations, participate in the maintenance process?

Two steps are recommended:

1. Define and document the maintenance stages of a the lifecycle model in detail.
2. Document the involvement of the appropriate operational managers in the context of the required lifecycle.

Later in this chapter, we give examples of how a procedure may be applied. The first example provided is based upon the change process detailed later in the change management section. Essentially, the example shows how to extend the change process description to include the design and development activities needed to implement a change (see Figure 13). Once the change process has been defined in more detail, it is then possible to identify and document the interactions between maintainers and operational management.

The second example relates to capacity management and includes interactions between SSADM and PRINCE2 or PMBoK (the Project Management Body of Knowledge from PMI, the Project Management Institute).

8.5 Application to Existing Services

Applying a new lifecycle model to an existing service may be difficult. It can be particularly challenging if the reasons for adopting a new model are to address problems such as poor service levels, low service availability, high capacity usage and excessive costs.

Applying a lifecycle model to an existing service raises a set of issues, which are different to those encountered in development. In particular:

- the existing lifecycle and requirements of the current IT infrastructure must be understood before a new model is introduced; no formally adopted lifecycle model may exist (a series of maintenance activities may have evolved into their current state)
- service levels must be maintained during the implementation
- customers must be involved in the planning and implementation of the new lifecycle model
- the contribution of operations management may be limited to key services, or to those which are currently available
- conflict between the relative documented priorities of the lifecycles needs to be identified
- implementation may have to be performed incrementally

It may be the case that a new lifecycle model is not required, but instead the existing lifecycle could be modified or improved. The guidance below can be applied to this scenario. Applying a new lifecycle model to an existing service requires the participation of maintainers, operational management staff and customers.

8.5.1 Documenting Operational Management Activities

To support the lifecycle model and subsequent processes, some form of illustration should be generated between lifecycle stages and operational IT management functions (note that the range of functions will almost certainly require expansion and at least proper application to your own circumstances). Figure 12 provides a suggested layout for a Service Design Activity Matrix (SDAM). This is, in fact, the first step in the generation of a process model, and the process model could be supplied to software developers for further expansion. The SDAM approach is one tool that you can use with regard to the issue of enterprise change management (you are taking an holistic viewpoint, integrating project management with change management activities throughout the lifecycle). Note that the axes can be used to map other frameworks; for example if audit of IT is likely to be an issue (as it is in large numbers of organizations), CobiT clauses could represent one axis and lifecycle stages another. It may be that ISO/IEC20000 is a goal, and so multiple matrices could be created, illustrating when attributes need to be considered during the lifecycle, or when infrastructure management processes are being designed, or as part of the stages of the project plan. In this way the SDAM is used as a series of checklists to ensure appropriate all-embracing issues are addressed.

The matrix (or matrices) would be initially presented as a blank layout. Interactions between operational management functions and various other activities are documented in the matrix. As a cross check on the content, software developers could perform, for example, a plotting exercise of their own for comparison.

The relationships to be plotted will vary for several reasons: for each lifecycle model, the 'lifecycle stage' axis would be likely to contain different stages and the order of work may vary, since each lifecycle model generates its own set of relationships. Within a specific lifecycle model there may be a number of variations with each variant causing changes to the matrix, and each IT service may have some characteristics which further modify the matrix.

The core objective is for planners and project managers to identify the relationships to enable effective operational management (configuration management).

Use the service functions included as a guide; templates are over used and their value is over estimated. The SDAM should always be created from first principles and emphasis placed on key process interfaces. In the new version of ITIL, you will see that processes once implicit are now explicitly called out (eg service catalog management and event management). Use these terms as you need to; similarly consider the issues of knowledge management and self help throughout (keep in mind that knowledge management as described elsewhere has a wider scope and intention).

Process/stage	I	F	R	S	P	C	U	Q	T	D	O	R
Capacity	=	=	=	=			=		=			
Cost	=			=							=	
Availablity	=			=	=	=	=	=	=	=		
SLM		=						=		=		=
Outsourcing												
Planning and Control	=			=		=						
Audit	=			=				=			=	
Customer Liaison	=	=							=			=
Disaster recovery				=					=		=	
Contingency planning				=					=		=	
Testing							=	=	=	=		
Release/SC&D												
Change						=	=	=	=	=	=	
Incident						=	=	=	=	=	=	
Problem						=	=	=	=	=	=	
Security	=		=					=			=	=
Configuration			=		=							
Computer operations		=					=	=	=	=		
Networks	=						=	=	=	=		
ITSDT	=	=	=	=	=	=	=	=	=	=	=	=
Catalogue	=		=						=	=		
etc												

- I Initiate
- F Feasibility study
- R Requirement analysis
- S Specification and design
- P Product/service design
- C Code
- U Unit testing
- Q Quality assurance
- T System testing
- D Deploy
- O Operate and maintain
- R Retire

Figure 12: An Example of a Completed Service Activity Design Matrix

Figure 12 shows the points of interaction at a high level, with software lifecycle stages. It will, of course, be necessary to describe this in more detail. SSADM is a method familiar to many software developers and this method is particularly suitable for enhancing the description. If multiple matrices are used (eg a CobiT vs SSADM, or PRINCE2 vs SSADM, or ISO/IEC 20000 vs ITIL for example) the same advice applies.

By decomposing stages to an appropriate level of detail it is possible to identify the precise involvement of auditors, developers, maintainers, operational managers and users at any point in the lifecycle. This type of illustration can be extended to include specific information about dependencies, staff involved and timescales.

How this information is represented is a matter of choice. An organization should use methods they are familiar with. These may include tables, data flow diagrams, flow charts and process diagrams; consistency is more important than choice of notation..

8.6 Change Management

A problem with many lifecycle models is that they do not describe the maintenance process in specific detail. In this next example, the waterfall model is mapped onto the main change management stages described in ITIL.

Figure 13 illustrates the main change management steps performed during each maintenance phase, and how these can be mapped onto the waterfall lifecycle model.

The aim is to satisfy two key objectives:

- Maintenance work is performed, as far as possible, using the same stage definitions as in development. This provides both continuity throughout the lifecycle in terms of methods and tools used by applying the same stages and activities and a tie-in to project management goals.
- The interactions between operational managers and maintainers can be planned and implemented using the same approach as for development.

Detailed planning of operational management interactions can be added (see Figure 13) in conjunction with the SDAM and the other techniques described earlier, to cover all interactions.

This example is based upon the assumption that the waterfall lifecycle model can be applied to maintenance. The entire waterfall must be transacted for each change, so a series of waterfalls make up the overall lifecycle.

There may be situations when radical new requirements may be specified for an existing service, and where there is uncertainty about the capacity of the service to cope with them. This illustrates both the complexity of the IT service design approach and the necessity to become capable in ITIL service delivery processes in order to address this type of issue. If this happens the waterfall model may be inappropriate, and the planning procedures in this book will be required to define an alternative. The new model will then have to be integrated into the change management process.

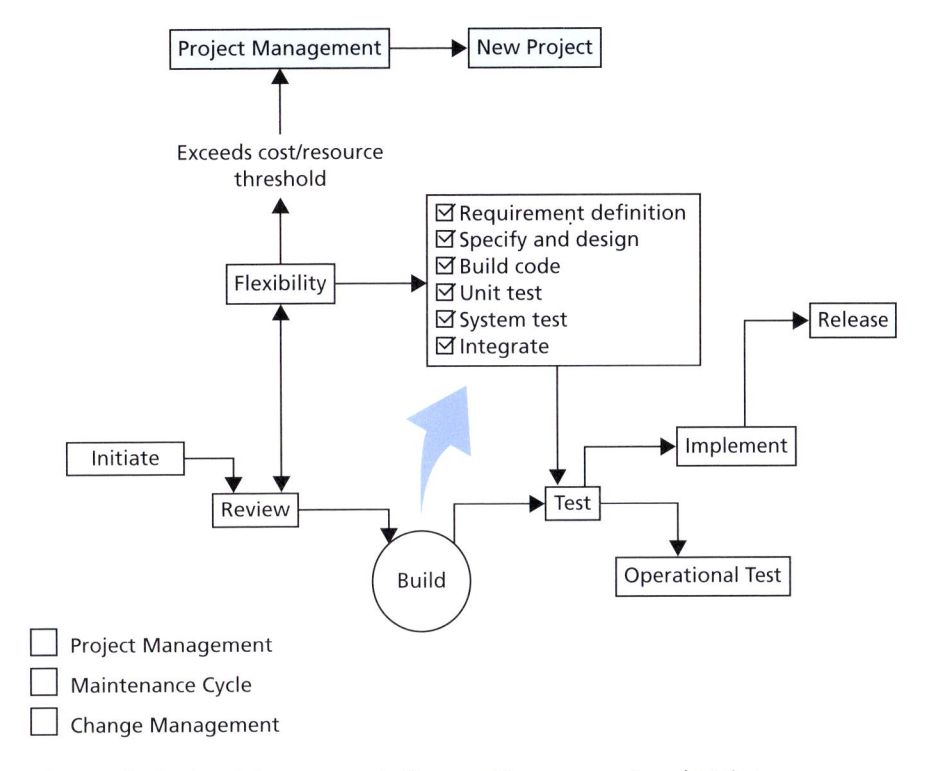

Figure 13: Project Management, Change Management and Maintenance

8.7 Capacity Planning and Structured Methods

For highly complex software services it may be necessary to develop a hybrid lifecycle model, or even multiple models.

This part of the book outlines the major interactions between the capacity management process and a selected lifecycle model. Generally, the choice of lifecycle model does not particularly affect the role of the capacity manager. Software developers *should* be aware of the needs of the capacity manager at the earliest possible stage in the development program. All too often, only cursory regard is given to the (potential) size of an IT service and the impact it will have on existing services running on the same IT infrastructure.

Structured methods concentrate on the functional definition of an information system and not necessarily a service *per se* (although some non-functional aspects are covered in detail). Keep in mind that a number of program specifications may be under development and a combination of the developments may become an IT service that is catalogued. SSADM is one example with interfaces to capacity management to address the needs of capacity planning. Most structured methods will have similar interfaces.

Systems analysis provides estimates for capacity management about, for example:

- probable hardware needs - to be ratified by capacity management
- workload types and workload volumes

The above information must be communicated to capacity management at various specified stages in structured analysis and design. Figure 14 illustrates the major interactions between customers, capacity planners and SSADM. It is not unusual for capacity managers to be unaware of the intended use of developments (in the preceding instance, the mix of IT services used by the business is more likely to be known by development and should be communicated to capacity planners to ensure that testing is a proper reflection of the live environment, rather than a simple load test of current services).

Another issue is the lack of awareness that change releases (either single RFC or multiple RFCs) may have on release of new applications/services.

With this approach, the impact of new developments on the live operations can be more accurately predicted. A smooth transition from development to live running, with forecasts about likely problems enabling operational managers to be proactive, becomes the normal way of working. Clearly, the usefulness of transitioning the Development Co-ordinator role to that of a live co-ordinator becomes apparent.

Similarly, in the maintenance process, if alterations to software are made, the capacity manager can model the effects on the IT infrastructure and make recommendations.

8.8 Impact

The capacity manager will be able to identify the effect of changes to software on other operational management functions. The capacity manager will also be aware of other projects using the techniques of lifecycle support and will be able to assess a number of options with different input scenarios. Software models of the existing IT services can be used to predict the effect of the changes. Conflicting developments (or developments involving RFCs) which are likely to create problems in capacity can be identified and plans made to reduce any unwanted impact.

The ability to identify and document interactions is crucial. The Program Support Office or an IT Planning Unit should be the focal point for the co-ordination of this information to capacity management, via the IT Service Co-ordinator.

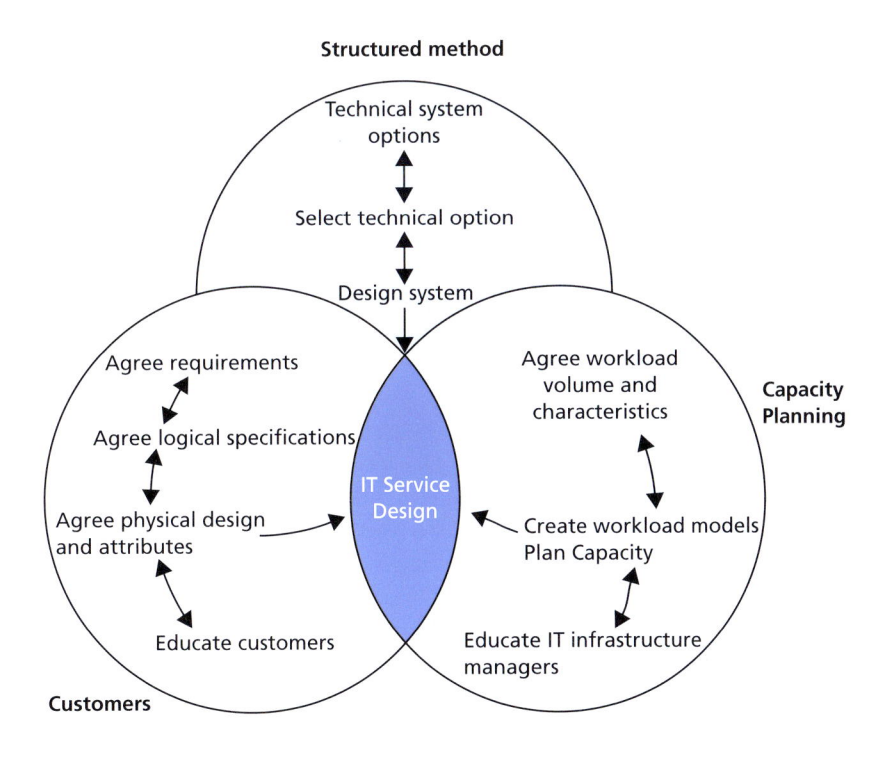

Figure 14: Example Methods Interactions

CHAPTER 9 Dependencies

This section provides guidance on identifying the dependencies to be considered when planning for lifecycle support from operational management staff. There is no definitive set of dependencies since each lifecycle model generates its own, and the dependencies may be method-specific, eg structured systems drivers.

One of the key objectives of IT is to improve the operational IT services delivered to customers. Key stakeholders to this continual improvement need are:

- the customer organization
- IT strategists
- operational managers
- software developers and maintainers

Commitment from these stakeholders needs to be enforced, from the Project Board for development projects, down to the project and stage managers.

The dependencies between operational management functions and the lifecycle model to be used in a given project should be planned. Figure 9 illustrates the relationships within the IT Board, and between the IT Board and the customer's business. With some interpretation this can lead to a complex set of dependencies which can be viewed in several ways:

- general dependencies, (including understanding the lifecycle and how it applies to operational management)
- for lifecycle support to begin, the operational management functions must be available, as illustrated in the SDAMs, and be ready to participate at different lifecycle stages
- there will be dependencies between the development team and the operational management functions within each lifecycle stage
- there will be interdependencies between individual operational management functions within each lifecycle stage
- there will be dependencies between operational management functions and the maintainers
- there will be dependencies between development team and the maintainers

IT can provide effective IT services to the customer organization if these dependencies are understood and are considered part of delivery.

Do not overlook general dependencies or service-specific dependencies. There may be many, including:

- individual IT service managers
- developers
- maintainers
- testers
- database and data dictionary administrators
- programmers
- technical support teams
- operations team
- project/program office
- design/standards office
- customers

9.1 Related Factors

Related factors which affect dependencies are:

- the need to provide IT services to support new development projects, (ie access to development software and tools) set by the development priorities
- the priority given to retrospective application of lifecycles to existing systems or services
- the requirement for dependent operational management functions such as change and configuration management, either to be implemented together, or for one service to be in place before another can begin

While these factors may determine the set of dependencies, there may be organizational constraints relating to budgets and resources which modify or perhaps override them.

It might not be necessary to implement the entire range of duties of a particular operational management function in order for lifecycle support to begin. For example, capacity management may be partially implemented early in the development lifecycle, with monitoring and control milestones scheduled for implementation when a service becomes operational.

The planning procedure described in Chapter Six will identify many of the dependencies through the use of the Service Design Activity Matrix and other tabulations created from the lifecycle model.

9.2 IT Service Co-ordinator

It is the IT Service Co-ordinator who will play the key liaison role with all of the people dependencies described earlier. This individual should be a manager within IT, ideally with experience in:

- software development
- software maintenance
- operational management
- lifecycle and process modeling
- quality assurance
- project planning techniques

In terms of personal skills, the IT Service Co-ordinator should have the following abilities:

- good communication skills, to communicate and promote the aims of co-ordinated development and software maintenance to a wide range of management and staff
- good planning and negotiating skills
- a diplomatic and practical approach to gain the acceptance of the many staff who will be affected
- the ability to manage without direct control, to motivate management and staff throughout the IT organization to fulfill their parts of the plans

The Development Co-ordinator will have the same attributes; the deputies may have less experience, but they should have potential to be senior managers in the organization.

9.3 Staffing Requirements

During the planning process, the impact of lifecycle support on the workload of operational management staff will need to be considered.

Staffing requirements can be assessed for each lifecycle stage, after analyzing the requirements of the stage. A further assessment of required skills is necessary at different stages of implementation.

The required team composition can then be crystallized. From this, any necessary changes to the composition of operational management teams can be identified. It will also be possible to determine where operational management staff perhaps needs to be included in the development or maintenance teams. Finally, additional training and education needs can be assessed.

9.4 Organizing Staff

It is difficult to give guidance on grades or skill levels for the individual roles, as there are too many dependent variables (geographically and organizationally) to make generalized guidance of any real value. However, the following guidance can be considered as guiding principles.

- The planning procedures will identify the operational management staff required at different lifecycle stages.
- The overall aim is to bring together groups of staff within an IT group who need to work together. The involvement of operational management staff should not appear to developers and maintainers as an imposition upon their work.
- It may be appropriate to organize multi-disciplinary teams, where operational management staff are co-opted for a specific lifecycle stage or period of time, to a development or maintenance team. During this time, the operational management staff will be required to perform the activities appropriate to each stage of the lifecycle. They may also be required to undertake parallel IT management activities in support of operational IT services.
- Specific operational management staff can be allocated to individual development projects as a consultancy resource, which can be called upon at the appropriate times to give operational management support.
- To increase the understanding of a co-ordinated approach to tasks undertaken by operational management staff, developers and maintainers, consideration should be given to rotating staff through these different areas of IT ('tours of duty').

9.5 When to Begin

If the organization is sufficiently mature (ie service delivery disciplines are in place and under control) and management is supporting the changes, the IT Service Co-ordinator should be appointed as soon as the decision has been made to implement lifecycle support.

It is likely that introduction will be oriented around specific events. The IT workload might consist of a mix of projects about to begin, development work which is at various stages of completion and services being maintained. This section considers the most appropriate time to implement full lifecycle support.

From a cost/benefit view, the ideal time for the introduction of lifecycle support is at the start of a major new project, when the greatest benefits can be realized.

However, it could be overly ambitious to try to implement lifecycle support in parallel with a major software development project, which may involve implementing new software technologies and techniques. An assessment of risk and project impact should be undertaken to ensure the appropriate course of action is followed.

The key consideration for the successful incorporation of lifecycle support into an organization is getting some 'quick wins on the board', where, once adopted, value and benefit are quickly apparent.

9.5.1 Pilot Projects

The recommended approach is to consider a pilot project for a new service (or phase of a service) where existing development practices are being used, and where the size of the project is manageable. Although the major benefits discussed earlier are unlikely to be realized using the pilot, there will be benefits:

- there will only be one major change, in terms of project management, which is the implementation of lifecycle support concepts
- a project of short duration will provide quicker feedback on successes and problems
- the operations management resources required will be relatively small
- the risk is reduced
- it should be easier to manage
- the experience gained can be used as input to further implementations

9.5.2 Existing Projects

An alternative approach is to consider a development project that is already under way. It may involve some significant re-planning of the project to enable all of the operational management teams to participate fully. The approach may be a more useful way of testing a more limited introduction of a service linked to lifecycle support where only a small number of IT infrastructure disciplines are involved.

For application to an existing service, the timing considerations must include:

- the remaining expected life of a service
- the anticipated degree of change during this life
- any problems related to maintainability
- impact on existing work effort

The introduction of new operational management disciplines (for example, the provision of an availability management function) will also determine the timing of additional training for lifecycle support.

Finally, timing will also depend upon organizational constraints, such as the availability of staff resources needed to implement plans, which is a common ongoing problem for any IT department.

CHAPTER 10 Embedding

10.1 Actions

The implementation or institutionalizing of lifecycle support will probably be rolled out over a period of time, and may involve specific projects or software developments in a phased, planned approach.

Implementation is concerned with:

- establishing the ITSDT
- appointment of the IT Service Co-ordinator
- success of the pilot project
- on-going application to projects and services

10.2 Running a Pilot Project

The IT Service Co-ordinator will play a major role in the roll out of the pilot project and needs to:

- co-ordinate software development plans and operational management plans for the duration of the pilot project
- ensure that all of the operational management teams are involved in the pilot project at the correct times, and that operational managers understand their individual roles (using the SDAMs as a guide)
- monitor and report on progress against the lifecycle support implementation plan
- ensure that problems are identified and resolved (if possible during the pilot)
- ensure that problems are not suspended in a 'pending' situation until the project evaluation review (be aware that in the pilot it may be necessary to do so with some problems that could jeopardize delivery)
- identify changes that need to be made to the plans and procedures during the project, and manage these changes
- assess the progress of the pilot against the original objectives, and, in particular, ensure that key metrics that illustrate benefits and costs are recorded
- ensure that the appropriate records are maintained by all of the operational managers involved, so that they are available at the project evaluation review

10.3 Dependencies

Dependencies should be identified for either of the following:

- introduction of lifecycle support using a pilot project
- introduction of lifecycle support across all of the software development projects

The key dependency in both however, is the availability of the IT Service Co-ordinator.

The other major dependencies are:

- the preparatory procedures required to introduce lifecycle support have been completed
- infrastructure managers are in place to manage service delivery processes
- a pilot project is available
- operational senior management is able and prepared to support the pilot project
- an awareness campaign has been undertaken to communicate what is to occur
- education and training needs of staff is understood and has been initiated

Once the pilot project has been completed and the benefit of lifecycle support is understood, the issues arising from the pilot can be reviewed with the objective of refining the plan to adopt and establish lifecycle support concepts and procedures. The introduction of lifecycle support to other projects in IT can then be undertaken, with the knowledge and experience from the pilot. The planning procedures described are generic, which means that once initial lifecycle models have been developed, they can be modified relatively quickly for new projects.

When the benefits of IT service design are better understood (for example, a noticeable improvement in the availability of new IT services following introduction), it will be easier to allocate resources for broader adoption.

The process of designing (and maintaining) a service catalog should also become less onerous, given the early involvement of the operational managers at the beginning of the design lifecycle.

The dependencies affecting on-going implementation are more likely to come from organizational constraints which limit the rate of extension of the revised working practices. Examples of those constraints are:

- insufficient operational management resources to support more than a given number of projects at any one time

- insufficient attention paid to ITIL service delivery processes
- the need to phase in specific operational management services as and when resources are available to implement them
- business pressure from the customer on the IT organization, which limits the degree of management support available for projects

10.4 People Involved

Implementation of the processes requires the involvement of operational management staff, developers and maintainers. This involvement increases as adoption grows.

The resource requirements for a project can be assessed during the planning phase; the Service Design Activity Matrix can be used as a guide to identify the staff from infrastructure management functions needed to support the different lifecycle stages.

One of the benefits of choosing a relatively small pilot project is that the number of staff involved will be limited. This will help to minimize the management problems of control and communication.

10.5 When to Take Action

With the IT Service Co-ordinator appointed, initial planning can start immediately and generic lifecycle models can be defined. An awareness campaign can be started to inform management and staff about lifecycle support and its importance to IT service design, as well as maintainability, reliability and resilience!

The timing of the introduction of lifecycle support into a pilot project should take into account:

- the need to begin the software project as soon as possible after an awareness campaign, in order to maintain the momentum
- introduction of new operational management functions which are needed to assist with the lifecycle support pilot project (do not underestimate the resources needed and the likelihood that experienced staff will be hard to find)
- availability of suitable staff
- the training requirements for the pilot team

As a guide, the elapsed time from the appointment of the IT Services Co-ordinator to the completion of a pilot project should be in the range of six to eighteen months. This range is suggested because the first attempts at introducing lifecycle support concepts and procedures to operational management and to a software development project should be considered as a short duration project. Keep in mind that many organizations are still struggling to introduce the ITIL process disciplines for projects that have been running for up to two years. Gaining control over delivery processes will require similar commitment and investment before they become sufficiently effective to be integrated with lifecycle support (let alone capable of designing an IT service).

The work undertaken to introduce lifecycle support in the pilot project is likely to raise issues that need resolution before starting incorporation into other projects. Early confirmation that the concepts and procedures are both practical and cost-effective (benefits are realizable) is essential for long-term success.

CHAPTER 11 Review and Audit

11.1 Actions

The following advice is for general consideration; the guidance is generic and can be viewed as the recommended regime for review of any operational management discipline. It is common to all types of ITIL projects.

11.2 Effectiveness and Efficiency Review

Many institutions regularly review IT services (periodically) to ensure that the organizational structure and methods continue to support the needs of the business. These reviews take the form of an effectiveness and efficiency study of the IT organization which covers:

- how efficiently it uses resources
- whether the individual and groups of functions perform effectively
- the effectiveness of information flows between functions and groups
- the effectiveness of customer relations

They should identify trends relevant to the way individual infrastructure management functions will be carried out in future. The concept should be extended to all organization types; the frequency of the reviews should be determined in consultation with the consumer of the IT services.

Audits are completed to determine and recommend the:

- existence of procedures
- compliance with (those) procedures
- improvements to existing procedures
- adoption of additional procedures

Ideally, audits should be independently conducted by audit teams from outside of the IT services organization. The separation of (appropriate) duties is essential with regard to compliance and, of course, the integrity of any IT service.

Where a quality management system (QMS) has been introduced (perhaps in line with quality management standards, such as ISO 9000/ISO 9001), quality audits must be planned to follow recommendations taken from the relevant standard.

The review of the pilot should be more focused, and it should be completed with understanding of the broader (or prospective) audit requirements.

Where organizations intend to achieve ISO/IEC 20000 certification, an external audit will be mandatory.

11.3 Project Success Review

The IT services manager is responsible for a co-ordinated approach to monitoring and reporting on the IT services organization. Projects that introduce changes to the organizational structure, such as lifecycle support, should be followed by project reviews which establish the success (or otherwise) of the project itself (against timescales, quality, costs, etc.) and of the changes it introduced (for example, meeting objectives for better customer liaison).

While responsibility for reviews of specific functions will remain with function managers, formal reviews should be co-ordinated in line with PMI or PRINCE2 recommendations. The instructions below are a summary of PRINCE2 recommendations.

The review plan should contain details of:

- Project Evaluation Reports (PER)
- Post-Implementation Reviews (PIR)
- Periodic Effectiveness and Efficiency Reviews (PEER)

Project Evaluation Reports (PERs) or Post-Implementation Reviews (PIRs) covering the introduction of lifecycle support should not wait until the entire lifecycle of any one project is complete, as a service may have a very long life. The guidance from ITIL recognizes decommissioning of a project or product may well be decades after creation. The reviews discussed here do not include the internal maturity assessment of individual process management functions.

11.4 Review of the Pilot Project

The key question which the Project Evaluation Review (PER) should answer is whether the introduction of IT Service Design processes has been successful. Planning for full implementation can only proceed if the pilot project has proved to be successful; lifecycle support can subsequently be extended to include other projects and planned (or existing) IT services.

The PER should cover the following:

- Were the terms of reference of the project met?
- Were costs within the budget estimates?
- What were the benefits that were recorded?
- What was the general conformance to the implementation plan, with particular regard to estimating, scheduling, meeting deadlines and use of resources?
- Were the dependencies pertaining to requirements for operational management identified in the SDAM?
- How easy or difficult was the management of the pilot, especially the need to co-ordinate the efforts of many different groups across the organization?
- Was quality management effective, both in terms of having procedures that were correct, and in terms of compliance with them?
- What problems were encountered during implementation of the pilot, and how were they resolved?
- What changes are recommended for the future, assuming that lifecycle support enabled service design is to continue?

The PER should include a recommendation to senior management on whether to proceed with the introduction of lifecycle support concepts and procedures. The recommendation should be supported by a cost/benefit case, based upon the pilot project, which should also detail the effectiveness of the operational process integration and the reliability of the services designed as a result of the work. The case must include specific metrics to be put in place.

11.5 Other Reviews

Whereas the PER of the pilot project is performed once, it is recommended that there are several stages where reviews of on-going activities may be required:

- following customer complaints at the end of a major delivery phase; for example, at the delivery of a service for operational testing
- after a major milestone; for example, acceptance of a service for live running periodically during maintenance

11.6 Responsibility

The IT services manager should be responsible for planning and performing reviews, but may select an independent person to undertake a review.

Internal quality audit staff or the ITSDT may be used to assist in this work. Consideration should be given to the skills required to perform these reviews. There are various review techniques, and it is an organizational choice as to which one is used. Most require an experienced chairman or moderator to control the review, to ensure that the right people are involved, to encourage participation, and ensure that the documented pre- and post-review procedures are followed.

CHAPTER 12 Benefits and Costs: The Good, the Bad and the Ugly

12.1 Benefits of a Pilot Project

The benefits of the introduction of lifecycle support concepts to facilitate and improve IT service design are discussed next in the following sections.

The first section examines the major benefits likely to accrue from a pilot project. The second section outlines the general benefits that IT may obtain. Some of the general benefits will also apply to the pilot.

The major benefit of a pilot project is to demonstrate to senior IT management that closer co-operation between operational management and development and maintenance personnel is both possible, and cost effective. This is achieved by demonstrating the practicability of introducing the co-operative processes and procedures and the resulting wider benefits for the business and IT.

A well selected pilot will enable senior management to exercise the procedures in this section, in a way that is controlled, and such that early results are possible. This is very important if the commitment of all those involved is to be sustained. While a successful pilot will record benefits relating to the specific project or service concerned, these are really secondary to establishing the practical viability of the concept.

12.2 Long-term Benefits

In contrast to the pilot project, where the major benefit was to prove the concept within a relatively short period of time, and of limited implementation scale, most of the benefits described in the following pages will accrue over an extended period of time.

Adoption of the principles of software lifecycle support allows IT to introduce quality procedures and address major security considerations emanating from the IS Strategy. Software lifecycle support will reinforce the ability of using structured methods to address these issues. In the long-term, it is cost-benefit that is the crucial factor. Built-in quality and security, reduced maintenance bills and improved delivery of IT services each contribute to a quality service. The customer of IT services should recognize an assurance that service levels are specified fully and achieved when a service becomes operational.

Meeting service level objectives in an efficient and timely way leads to three financial benefits:

1. Internal operating costs are reduced due to more efficient use of IT resources to support the information services.
2. Improved service levels mean greater customer satisfaction, and this, in turn, will provide further opportunity to invest in other process improvement initiatives.
3. Since maintainability is a design goal throughout the lifecycle, there will be a better match of requirements and operational resources, which will result in lower operational and maintenance costs.

Reduction in costs can be reflected in reduced charges to customers, to the benefit of the business. For IT there are also benefits in terms of culture. In tandem with other operational management disciplines, lifecycle support contributes to:

- making the best use of costly human resources, removing communication barriers, such as those that can exist between developers and maintainers within IT, or between the IT group and the customer
- promoting the idea that the organization is a team made up of groups acting together to meet the common goal of customer satisfaction with IT services, which will foster greater mutual understanding
- developing a quality obsessed culture, where the aim of IT is to meet the customer need

12.3 Costs

When considering the issue of costs it is important to remember that software maintenance accounts for a significant proportion of IT expenditure in a typical IT organization. The benefits accruing from a co-ordinated approach to development and maintenance should result in overall cost savings, and more than compensate for costs incurred. It is important to recognize that the benefits and savings may accrue over a long period of time. Project portfolio management techniques can be gainfully employed here to provide accurate metrics.

The main costs of establishing the role of the ITSDT relate to employment costs (the IT Service Co-ordinators and/or any liaison officers, and any increase to the IT Planning Unit complement), plus those for project management and lifecycle modeling tools. Given the market acceptance of ITIL processes, a large (probably unanticipated) investment in service delivery processes will be needed.

The implementation of the concepts raises a number of other cost issues. They include:

- awareness campaigns and training programs, where the expense will be a combination of course development and staff time
- costs of implementation, which will vary with different lifecycle models, and during the stages of a lifecycle
- costs to support individual projects and the effects on budgets; in approximate terms, this could add between 5%-20% to development costs (bear in mind that up-front expenditures are an investment which serve to reduce operation and maintenance costs, which are the dominant factors in overall lifecycle costs)
- identifying ways of measuring the actual costs of a wide range of operational management functions, so that the costs can be consolidated in a meaningful way
- determining how costs are to be treated (eg overhead or rechargeable to customer groups)
- how costs should be included in cost/benefit models; project portfolio management is, of course, a key factor in this area

12.4 Possible Problems

There is always distrust of, and resistance towards change. Altering the relationships between operational management, consumers of IT services, and software developers and maintainers represents significant change. The nature of the changes themselves, and asking people to work together in new ways, may increase such concerns. For example, if the developers perceive closer co-operation with operational management as an intrusion or threat, they may resist (and if ITIL is forced upon them, resistance will be inevitable).

Since its introduction, few have resisted introduction of ITIL as ardently as IT developers, and with good cause. ITIL is not a development method, and development has never been involved in creation of processes that they consider relevant in that domain. Attempting to impose, for example, ITIL change management procedures on development does not work because the work methods, impact and needs are very different. IT needs to find a suitable champion for the introduction of lifecycle support. The selection of the IT Service Designer/Co-ordinator is critical. This is not a trivial task, as an effective champion needs a number of skills and attributes including:

- authority
- belief in the new concepts
- enthusiasm
- accepted credibility
- the ability to persuade others

And, as always, high quality people will be in demand throughout the organization: can such a person be placed in this role and, if so, at what expense?

It will undermine the credibility of the implementation if the individual promoting lifecycle support and IT service design is not a true advocate of the approach.

Lifecycle support is a complex subject involving many people, and so there must be documented ownership of the changes to working practices (and as we have discussed, documentation runs counter to many RAD methods). Individual managers should be able to clearly identify their responsibilities. Failure to ensure that the responsibilities are made clear and accepted will lead to a vague and ineffective collective responsibility.

Changes may be required to long-standing working practices. For example, teams which traditionally worked independently now have to work in unison with other groups within IT. Managers will need to use care and sensitivity in explaining the needs for change and the benefits to their staff, otherwise staff may see the changes as a threat.

CHAPTER 13 Technology Support

13.1 Tools for the IT Service Co-ordinator

Implementing lifecycle support implies some degree of integration of tools. This is considered for:

- software tools for the IT Service Co-ordinator
- software tools for operational managers
- software tools for development and maintenance teams
- project portfolio management

The IT Service Co-ordinator will need software tools commonly used in IT Planning Units. The most important of these is a project portfolio management tool which can be used to develop generic project plans for lifecycle support and IT service design. There may be different plan formats to support different lifecycle models. Usually, one of these plans will be selected and modified for a specific project.

Project management tools are widely used and should be adequate for this task; however, they are frequently used stand-alone. Portfolio management tools are often more appropriate to track overall investments in multiple projects. The IT Service Co-ordinator needs to amalgamate plans for software development projects with operational management plans. The process of integrating lifecycle support provides a good opportunity to consider development of a shared or networked planning environment and may offer an effective approach to integrating the plans of operational management, development and maintenance teams.

The IT Service Co-ordinator may require tools for modeling lifecycles, and decomposing them to show tasks, activities, dependencies, deliverables and staffing requirements. There is a wide choice in the marketplace and it rests largely on personal preference and/or organizational policies.

As the lifecycle models and modeling process become better understood, an advanced approach may be applied, such as using an analyst workbench, and notations such as data flow diagrams (DFDs). DFDs have the advantage that underlying relationships can be defined and maintained. There are also a number of powerful tools available to software developers to facilitate process modeling.

13.2 Tools for Operational Management

From the modeling and planning process, it will be possible to identify where tools may improve the operational management work.

The plans will show operational management tasks, and may be annotated to indicate the most manually intensive tasks. The current use of software tools can be mapped onto a plan, so that it is possible to identify the potential for further automation. For example, only performance management tools may be in current use in the organization. The plan may cater for the organization to expand the use of tools, to include service level monitoring tools which are often linked to performance management tools and, at a later stage, to capacity management tools.

13.3 Tools for Development and Maintenance Teams

The development and maintenance teams require tools for the storing of software artifacts, version control, configuration and build management. Linkage of these tools in various 'integrated development environments', and integration with the tools used by the IT Service Co-ordinator and operational managers, will drive significant quality improvements and efficiency gains, in addition to the governance benefits.

13.4 Tools for Project and Portfolio Management

The importance of project and portfolio management should not be overlooked; many consider project and portfolio management as the glue that holds everything together.

The business challenges in investing in any IT initiative are simple:

- cost control
- risk management
- alignment of IT services to business needs
- optimising the provision of IT services

With the right project and portfolio management tools, these challenges can be managed and reported on more effectively. Specifically, the following require consideration:

- linkage of standards (CobiT, ISO/IEC 20000, etc.) to process execution steps
- auditability and traceability of process execution
- consistent and template driven IT planning and budgeting

- IT services linked to business aligned IT portfolios (eg single invoices for the capture of costs as they pertain to the provision of IT services)
- incremental measurement of benefits against IT services
- agility in reallocating resources as business priorities change
- 'what if' analysis capability scenarios to assess impact of reallocation/reprioritisation of IT resources/services

We have mentioned throughout this book that most organizations are currently in the throes of procuring/implementing service support software to automate activity and enforce consistent process execution. In addition, many organizations are also implementing technologies that manage the processes that feed in and out of the service lifecycle:

- security management
- governance and compliance
- application management
- software change management
- IT asset management
- project and portfolio management

IT efficiency has a linear relationship to the level of integration between all IT resources; in order for full value to be extracted from any IT investment, it is essential that interdependencies are known and understood, and the right priority is set for all activities. It can be argued that, before any IT efficiency initiative is undertaken or any activity commences, the control and measurement framework should be put in place.

If the appetite for true IT transformation exists within an organization, careful consideration should be given to aligning all of these disciplines under a single enterprise IT management suite, whereby automation and integration of these disciplines can be deployed efficiently by leveraging 'out of box' integrations, while reducing implementation risks/costs and driving down medium to long-term operational costs.

Annex One: Definitions and Abbreviations

Adaptive maintenance	Adapting a service to fit an improved hardware or software environment.
ASD	Adaptive Software Development.
ASL	Application Services Library: a library initiated by the Dutch Ministry of Defense.
CGI	Computer-generated imagery.
CI	Configuration Item.
CMDB	Configuration Management Database.
CMM	Capability Maturity Model.
COCOMO	Constructive Cost Modeling.
COM	Computer Operations Management.
Corrective maintenance	The provision of the management, operation and support of an organization's computers and/or networks by an external source at agreed service levels. The service will generally be provided for a set time at an agreed cost.
COSO	Committee of Sponsoring Organizations of the Treadway Commission.
COTS	Commercial off the shelf: Shrink-wrapped components.
CobiT	Control Objectives for Information and Related Technology.
DFD	Data Flow Diagrams.
DSDM	Dynamic Systems Development Method.
FDD	Feature Driven Development.
FM	Facilities Management.
FPA	Function Point Analysis: An application-independent measure of a program size.
HLS	High Level Schedules.
ICT	Information and Communications Technology.
ISO/IEC 20000	International standard for IT Service Management.
ISO/IEC 27000	In ternational standard for information security.
ITIL	IT Infrastructure Library.
ITSC	IT Service Co-ordinator.
ITSDT	IT Service Design Team: Manage the day-to-day interfaces between the business side, development, testing, technical services - such as database design and administration - and operations.

IT Service Analyst	The individual who is responsible for co-ordinating operation management activities within the various software developments.
IT System	In the context of this book, IT system is used as an embracing term for the hardware and software that serve as the basis for provision of an IT service or service to customers.
ITT	Invitation To Tender.
Legacy	The term used to describe services or systems which have been in use for many years.
Lifecycle	In the context of this book, lifecycle is an abbreviation for software lifecycle.
LSDM	Learmonth Structured Development Method.
Maintainability	This is the attribute of a service which reflects how easily it can be changed.
Maintenance	Correcting errors or bugs in software.
OLA	Operational Level Agreements.
Outsourcing	The complete environment needed for maintaining services, including hardware, software, methods, tools, organization, staff, and IT infrastructure. See also 'Facilities Management'.
PDCA Cycle	'Plan-Do-Check-Act Cycle of Continuous Improvement.
PER	Project Evaluation Reports/Reviews.
PEER	Periodic Effectiveness and Efficiency Reviews.
Perfective Maintenance	Changing a service to meet new functional requirements, or enhancing the service.
PIR	Post-Implementation Reviews.
PMI	Project Management Institute; also refers to their own established project management methodology, including PMBoK, the Project Management Body of Knowledge.
Preventative Maintenance	A set of related activities, seen as a coherent process subject to measurement, involved in the production of a model of the service which can then be altered or enhanced.
PRINCE2	*PRojects IN Controlled Environments*: A project management methodology, covering the management, control and organization of a project.
Program	A group of projects that are managed together in a co-ordinated way, in order to gain business benefits which may not be possible if the projects were managed independently.

QIP	Quality Improvement Programs.
QMS	Quality Management System.
QMFITS	Quality Management for IT Services.
RAD	Rapid Application Development methods.
Re-engineering	The process of (optionally) re-constructing the design of a service (reverse engineering) and enhancing and re-implementing that design either in a different environment or in order to produce more efficient and/or effective software.
Reverse engineering	The process of re-constructing (a part of) the design of a service from program code (source or compiled).
RFC	Request(s) for Change.
RUP	Rational Unified Process.
SAP	Systems, Applications and Products in Data Processing:Enterprise Resource Planning software.
SC&D	Software Control and Distribution.
Scrum	System Configuration Recovery Utilization and Methodology.
SDAM	Service Design Activity Matrix.
SDLC	Software Development Lifecycle: The period of time that begins with the decision to develop a software product and ends when an acceptable product is delivered.
SLM	Service Level Management.
Software	A generic term for those components of a computer system (eg a program), which are intangible rather than physical. A distinction is drawn between systems software (which is an essential component to the hardware, and most often supplied by the hardware manufacturer) and an applications service (which is specific to the role performed by the computer in a given organization).
Software Engineering	The entire range of activities used to design and develop software.
Software Lifecycle	The entire lifetime of an IT service, from initial conception to final decommissioning. It includes enhancement and maintenance following delivery.

Software Lifecycle Model	A model used to plan the work for an IT service, so that activities take place, in the right order, and in a way that minimizes risk and increases quality. A software lifecycle model captures: • the major activities to be completed • the logical dependencies between them • the products resulting from the major activities
Software Maintenance	The modification of a software product after delivery, to correct faults, improve performance or other attributes, or to adapt the product to a changed environment.
Software Method	A systematic way of performing part or all of the processes involved in a lifecycle model or stage (for example, the requirements stage, or design stage, etc).
Software Product	A software entity (a program or suite of programs).
Software Prototyping	The development of a preliminary version of a service in order to allow certain aspects of that service to be investigated (often to elicit early feedback about functionality from potential users, or to test technical feasibility).
Software System	One or more applications developed to perform a business function.
SSADM	Structured Systems Analysis and Design Method.
TQM	Total Quality Management.
XP	Extreme Programming.
Yourdon	Edward Nash Yourdon, lead developer of the structured systems analysis and design method (SSADM).

Annex Two: Summary of the Principal IT Service Design Process Steps

- Create a team to manage the liaison between development and operations.
- Identify and document an accurate understanding of the required attributes of the new IT service.
- Working with the customer, development and operations; create an outline SDAM.
- Create a project (or program) plan depending on the scale of the work.
- Establish roles and responsibilities.
- Document all steps and stages (including decommissioning), models and methods to be used or referenced and flesh out the SDAM.
- Determine expected service levels, capacity and availability requirements, anticipated costs and charges, and plans to ensure service in the event of disaster.
- Ensure appropriate involvement as design, specification, coding and testing is undertaken by development.
- Build a service design plan that includes quality, compliance, security resource and metrics tracking.
- Create a plan for the deployment and maintenance of the new service, ensuring all necessary IT infrastructure/operations interfaces are fully understood and that roles have been allocated where gaps were identified.
- If required, cross-train development and operations teams to ensure a common understanding.
- Ensure all business approvals, budgets, etc., are in place.
- Begin the procurement process for any required hardware or software based on the analysis of the new services.
- Determine service support roles required (incident, problem, change, configuration and release manager roles) and identify responsibilities during testing and handover activities.
- If necessary, procure and install management tools needed (eg project portfolio management to track projects and costs, CMDB to track assets and CIs).
- Establish control and co-ordination of project management and request for change (RFC) processes.
- Test the services as appropriate.
- Ensure any operational procedures are documented and that customers have been fully trained in the use of the new services.
- Deploy the services.

- Carry out reviews as appropriate to establish that the service functions as was specified.
- Review the effectiveness of the lifecycle models in reducing cost of maintaining the new services.

Annex Three: Procedures for Application to Existing Services

Introduction

Applying the processes of lifecycle support to an existing service is a complex task which raises three immediate questions:

- Is there a business case to support the process?
- What degree of integration is needed and how should this be developed?
- Are there maintainability issues which have an impact on management of the operational and prompt a need for improvement work?

Document and Assess the Current Situation

In order to determine whether there is a business case for change, it is necessary to document the current situation in the following ways:

The lifecycle stages or model being used should be formalized. Particular attention should be paid to the interfaces between customers of IT services, maintenance functions and operational management. All methods and tools being used to support the current model should be identified and recorded.

Project management methods used to support the model should be documented. This is often a weak area in existing maintenance and requires careful attention. The reason for this is that maintenance can be viewed as a continuous flow of work, rather than a discrete project. Operational management must manage both the operational service and the flow of changes to the services.

The procedures described in Chapter Five should be used to assess the effectiveness of the current lifecycle model and its ability to underpin lifecycle support within the maintenance stages.

These analyses will give pointers to the interactions between the operational managers and where the software maintenance processes require strengthening.

Software maintenance managers have to measure those aspects of performance which may identify the need to improve software lifecycle support. They include:

- the annual change traffic on the service, expressed in terms of number and sizes of changes
- the productivity achieved with the current model and the ability of maintainers to deliver change to meet business schedules
- the inherent maintainability of the application as expressed in terms of:
  - design characteristics, which help or hinder change to the service
  - the reliability and stability of the service as measured by the numbers and types of failures

From this information, an assessment can be made of the overall effectiveness of the current model and its infrastructure support. A case can then be built for further implementation. If serious deficiencies are found from these analyses, then the next phase is to plan the implementation of a new or enhanced lifecycle support strategy.

Enhancing Strategies

To achieve this, it is recommended that the planning procedures outlined earlier are applied, but with modifications. The major planning steps are:

- the assessment of alternative lifecycle models which can be applied to the maintenance stages
- the derivation of a SDAM to show how the operational management functions will interact with the new or enhanced model (see Chapter Eight)
- use of the generic planning procedures documented in Chapter Six to demonstrate how each individual operational management function will interact with the model
- identification of new methods and tools required to support the new model
- identification and planning for the implementation issues, such as the maintaining of service levels, or the need for incremental implementation
- determining training needs for maintainers and service staff
- estimating the costs of implementation and operation of the new support strategy, and the benefits and risk associated with it

Improvement Work Required for a New Lifecycle Strategy

The inability of operational management to deliver an acceptable operational service may not just stem from inadequate lifecycle support. A major cause may be that a service is becoming inherently un-maintainable. Changes to operational management support alone may be insufficient.

In conjunction with the planning for improved lifecycle support, it may be necessary to plan remedial work to the service. This work may involve the following tasks:

- analysis of documentation, followed by re-documentation of key areas
- re-engineering of programs which are both difficult to change and that are subject to most changes, where re-engineering may involve the complete rewriting of programs
- reverse engineering of databases to identify and remove any forms of data complexity or deadly embraces, which lead to poor maintainability

Detailed discussion of improvement projects of this nature are outside the scope of this book. From the planning perspective, it is recommended that the standard approach proposed in the module is used. For example, if programs are to be re-engineered there is a requirement to:

- document the re-engineering lifecycle stages
- determine an SDAM showing where operational management interacts with re-engineering lifecycle stages, bearing in mind that the lifecycle may be very similar to that of new development

If significant re-engineering work is to be undertaken, operational management may be concerned with issues such as:

- whether the reliability and functions of the re-engineered code can meet service level agreements
- the operational testing of re-engineered code
- the effects of re-engineered programs on capacity management

Annex Four: Impact on Specific Infrastructure Management Activities

Introduction

This annex describes the most prominent operational management functions in general terms, so as to provide an appreciation of how they are affected by an integrated approach. Numerous publications have been devoted to these functions, and some of them are referred to in this section.

The aim is to define briefly the purpose of each operational management function, and to identify some of the key planning and implementation issues which need to be addressed.

Figure 15 describes the principal ITIL processes/functions, and where they fit into organization maturity models as strategic, tactical or operational.

For many operational management functions it may be possible to develop generic descriptions of how a specific function interacts with a particular lifecycle model. These descriptions can then be tailored to meet the needs of an individual project. However, care should be taken to assess each project fully, so that existing descriptions are not simply assumed to be the correct ones.

The Business Perspective

The ITIL Business Perspective series aimed to elevate strategic thinking about IT and information systems in general, to business people familiar with technology, but with little interest or regard for its value or criticality.

Where it was adopted, the benefits realized included board level members discussing IT investments critically and making informed decisions about the role of IT as a critical business support mechanism. Where it was not adopted, IT remained largely a commodity like any other. While IT is not 'special' and deserves no more attention than other critical support functions, its complexity should cause consideration as should its ubiquity.

The Business Perspective series was compiled from a business standpoint, not from the point of view of IT telling the business what to do. The interactions between customers, developers and operations was discussed in scenarios ranging from mergers and acquisitions to computer desktop upgrades, and examples provided of where the business could reasonably focus attention to bring benefit to the organization when IT projects were undertaken.

Strategic Goals

- Quality Management
- Application Lifecycle Support
- IT Service Design (including policies and architecture)
- Planning and Control
- Capacity Management
- SLM

Tactical Goals

- Customer Liaison
- Supplier Liaison (including FM, Third Party Maintenance)
- Cost Management for IT
- Business Continuity / Contingency Planning
- Availability Management

Operational Goals

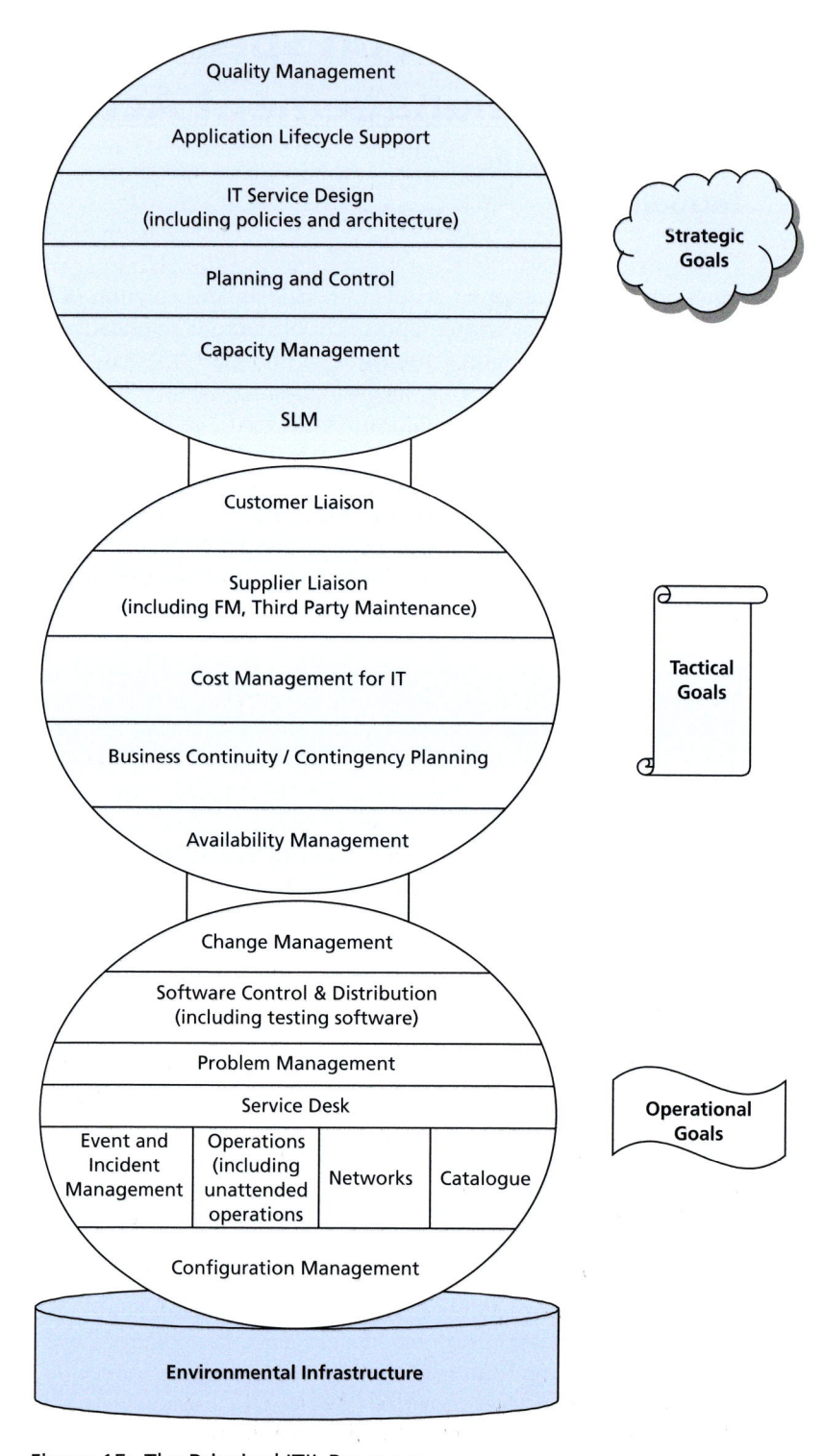

- Change Management
- Software Control & Distribution (including testing software)
- Problem Management
- Service Desk
- Event and Incident Management
- Operations (including unattended operations)
- Networks
- Catalogue
- Configuration Management

Environmental Infrastructure

Figure 15: The Principal ITIL Processes

Lifecycle support clearly plays into the same space, but at a level of detail that is more suitable to senior managers and their teams than to the board of directors. However, the examples used in the books (and the checklists of ideas) remain useful as pointers to the sort of improvements to IT service provision and maintainability that could reasonably be sought by businesses in full control of their IT department.

Customer Liaison

In many respects, customer liaison is met by the ITSDT, though ITIL does not properly address the organizational issues required to join up the development and operations domains. It is strong in the support of effective liaison with customers being essential to a better return on IT investment and of education of those customers in making better use of IT. The advice in the book is useful with regard to improving customer relationships, traditionally a weak spot for operations, and it can be used in tandem with this book to join together the concepts that make the customer, development and operations liaisons an even more effective goal.

Planning and Control for IT Services

It is assumed that planning and control mechanisms are already present within an organization. The purpose of planning and control is to ensure that individual operational management function plans can be integrated to accommodate the needs of an overall IT service plan, and that they do not conflict with one another; the plans must be comprehensive, co-ordinated and coherent.

There are strong links between planning and control and infrastructure planning. It also has particular relevance to:

- base level operational plans, which describe the overall budgets, resources, accommodation and IT capacity required
- plans for individual IT services (ie services delivered to the customer), describing objectives such as availability targets, budgetary limits and service level targets

The co-ordination task is to:

- ensure that operational managers prepare plans for specific projects
- integrate those plans into the base level operational plan, and resolve any conflicts
- monitor the implementation and progress of the IT service plans as the lifecycle stages are actioned
- ensure that any changes to these plans are checked against the base plan
- provide management reports to both the head of IT services and to the project board

Quality Management for IT Services (QMFITS)

The QMFITS book examined operational functions in relation to the ISO 9001 standard, providing advice on how organizations could use ITIL to help them obtain ISO 9001 certification. The QMFITS module also describes the audit of operational management processes and products against standards and procedures. For any organization wishing to implement formal quality assurance, QMFITS is the essential function which advises management upon effectiveness of their quality systems.

In terms of planning for lifecycle support, the quality manager role will need to:

- define the quality management system to be used to support the software lifecycle, which may be based upon ISO9001
- determine the quality plan for each project, covering all stages from feasibility study through to maintenance

There may be significant variation in the application of quality procedures to different lifecycle models. For example, using the waterfall model to develop new IT services will require quality procedures in all development stages. By comparison, quality procedures might be difficult to apply in prototyping or simulation environments used in other lifecycle models. In this case, it is necessary to define clearly the point at which quality procedures are applicable to software being developed in this way. The exact application of quality procedures is documented in the project quality plan.

Managing Facilities Management

In general, the use of any third party in part or all of a service lifecycle will have an impact on lifecycle support. There may be many possible relationships between Facilities Management (FM) or outsourcing and the operational management disciplines. The 'Understanding and Improving' book from ITIL version 1 is a good reference source for assistance in defining roles.

Figure 16 shows how responsibility for providing operational management functions may be transferred to an FM provider. The diagram shows how the operational management function is split from the in-house organization and run by the FM supplier.

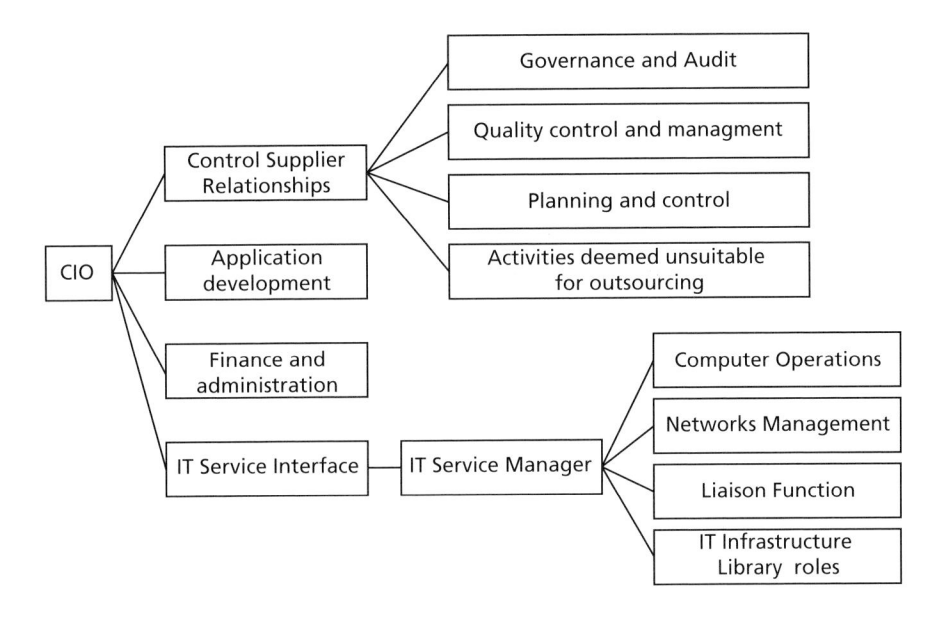

```
                                    ┌─ Governance and Audit
                                    │
                   Control Supplier ─┼─ Quality control and managment
                   Relationships    │
                  ╱                 └─ Planning and control
                 ╱   Application    ─── Activities deemed unsuitable
    CIO ───────┼─── development         for outsourcing
                ╲
                 ╲  Finance and                        ┌─ Computer Operations
                  ╲ administration                     │
                                                       ├─ Networks Management
                    IT Service Interface ─ IT Service Manager
                                                       ├─ Liaison Function
                                                       │
                                                       └─ IT Infrastructure
                                                          Library roles
```

Figure 16: Common responsibilities in ITSM after outsourcing

There are several possible variations on the use of Facilities Management (FM), which include:

- all lifecycle activities performed by the FM provider, with delivery of all IT services also contracted out, development performed in-house, with in-house maintenance services to support
- operation and maintenance performed by a third party, with its own operational development performed by a third party, but using in-house operational resources
- maintenance performed by a third party also using in-house operational management

Wherever a third party or FM provider is used, the in-house organization will require some form of liaison with the contractor.

For lifecycle support planning, the use of a third party does not necessarily change the Service Design Activity Matrix relationships for a given lifecycle model. However, it will involve different people.

The selected lifecycle model and the support services identified therein are used to control and manage any third party contracts. The model is also used in the procurement of turnkey services. The requirements of implementing the model are used within an 'Invitation To Tender' (ITT) to specify methods of working, and the quality and project management systems to be used during project work. Also, they can be used to specify the interfaces between the personnel of each company, as a basis for planning and implementing work units, and for defining deliverables. A further use is to provide the standards for the audit of a third party, ensuring that it conforms to contractual requirements.

Cost/ Financial Management for IT Services

Irrespective of using the terms cost or financial management for IT services, this section describes the costing of and charging for IT services to customers. In service lifecycle terms this may be:

- the costs and charges relating to the development of services
- the costs and charges relating to on-going operation and maintenance of services

Financial management is active in all lifecycle stages. In summary, the financial manager participates in:

- planning the financial management approach towards development
- providing financial management services to monitor development costs
- planning the financial management services required for operation and maintenance
- providing financial management services for operation and maintenance

The effect of different lifecycle models upon the cost management process is likely to be small. The reason for this is that while costs attributable to different stages of the lifecycle may be recharged to different budgets, an organization still has to collect data on and account for, all costs incurred during the lifecycle.

Once more, the principal issue is the lack of investment in this discipline in the majority of organizations.

Service Level Management (SLM)

Service Level Management (SLM) describes the function which is responsible for ensuring that the required operational service levels are provided to the customers within an organization. It is a key operational management function.

To achieve this, service level managers must be actively involved, both during development and maintenance stages. Operational Level Agreements (OLAs) and Service Level Agreements (SLAs) have to be specified during the development stages so that acceptance tests can be designed which validate the requirements. Service levels have subsequently to be monitored and maintained during operation. In particular, changes to any operational service, whether software or hardware, may affect overall machine loading and have an impact on the service levels of other services.

In general terms, service level management will be involved in the following lifecycle stages:

- in feasibility studies, where initial advice may be sought about desirable service levels or a proposed service
- during requirements definition, where initial service level objectives can be defined
- during overall services design, where architectural constraints may impact achievable service levels, and when compromises may be needed
- during system, acceptance and user testing, when it will be shown whether a service is capable of meeting SLAs
- in an on-going role during the operational life of a service (ie maintenance)

If the lifecycle model being used involves risk assessments and prototyping, then service level staff may be involved in additional tasks. For example, they may be asked to assess alternative design approaches to determine which ones will best meet service level requirements.

Capacity Management

Capacity management is concerned with ensuring that computer capacity can meet the requirements of an organization. It is much more than performance management and will require considerable investment in most organizations, to bring the function and processes up to the CMM 'control' level 3 that is the minimum requirement in order to be successfully involved in lifecycle support activities.

As with service level management, this function should be involved in the lifecycle at the earliest stage possible. The key elements of capacity management are:

- business capacity planning
- storage management
- demand management
- system and IT service sizing
- performance management
- workload management

Ensuring that there is sufficient capacity to meet service levels is an essential task. To achieve this, capacity management must be very well integrated with the development and maintenance stages.

For example:

- capacity planners will be involved in feasibility studies; assessing in general the capacity implications of proposed services, and their effects on existing ones
- during the specification and design stages, capacity planners will be developing detailed estimates of the various hardware resources required to provide the anticipated service levels
- in acceptance testing, capacity management staff will need to verify that the actual resources required are within the bounds of the planned values (and available resources)
- during operational service and maintenance, capacity management will be concerned with ensuring that services have appropriate levels of resource

Capacity management may have different levels of involvement with different lifecycle models. The waterfall model supports capacity planning in the earlier development stages, on the assumption that requirements can be fixed at an early stage. With the spiral model, capacity planning may not be possible until much later in the lifecycle, when the requirements have been finally agreed and any risks resolved.

Disaster Recovery and Business Continuity Planning

Irrespective of what to call any of the activities related to recovering IT services following a major outage (contingency planning, business continuity planning, disaster recovery, you select your favorite!), the issue is that important IT services must be restored securely to the business in the minimum time possible. This will necessitate looking at options such as cold or hot start-up, duplicate sites, etc., all with focus on the priority of which IT services should be recovered first and, the real nub of the issue, how much it will cost.

To integrate this discipline with the service lifecycle, consideration should be given to the following:

- actionable contingency plans are needed from the start of development for the recovery of the project environment, and the continuation of development work following a disaster
- operational contingency needs have to be captured at the software requirements stage, so that their impact on service design and implementation can be assessed
- during systems testing, contingency plans need to be exercised
- at handover, all operational business and IT contingency planning must be complete and verified

Disaster or contingency plans require regular revision as new services are developed.

Availability Management

The availability management function is concerned with providing high levels of reliability, serviceability and availability of IT services to customers. The function is crucial to underpin service level agreements.

Availability management in the context of this book encompasses three major tasks:

- planning and managing the reliability and availability of services that will meet SLAs
- collaborating with other operational management functions, eg problem management, proactively to improve service reliability beyond the minimum level of SLA
- overseeing contractual reliability and serviceability of supplied and maintained components and services

In all of these tasks, a major component, and one which is not easy to address, is that of software reliability.

Availability management functions need to be involved during both development and maintenance stages. During the early development stages it is necessary to define the required reliability. During testing for operational use, the availability manager will want to monitor the actual reliability of a new service against the values needed to underwrite the SLAs. Finally, during operation and maintenance, it is necessary to maintain records of reliability, growth or decay.

A key function of availability management is not only to measure current software reliability, but to identify trends. This is applicable in both development and maintenance. Consequently, the availability manager will work closely with the service level and problem managers.

For example, from records of errors found during development, it may be possible to produce statistical predictions of improving reliability. These may be valuable indicators for determining when, and even if, a service will meet its reliability specification.

In the maintenance phase, software reliability may change in different ways. A service may stabilize and become very reliable. Alternatively, reliability may decay as an increasing number of changes render the source code more fragile.

As high reliability is an inherent measure of the quality of a service, it is clear that, whatever lifecycle model is used, it must support good design and coding practices. Availability management staff should therefore have an involvement in the methods and tools used by systems developers.

Here again, a very high degree of maturity in the discipline is required in order to properly enable involvement to the betterment of IT service design. Very few organizations currently demonstrate such maturity, and for those interested in becoming version 3 'conformant' this is, and will continue to be, a major hurdle.

Configuration Management and Change Management

These processes are very often implemented concurrently because of their interdependence. The grouping of them either in the service support lifecycle, or as they are in ITIL version 3, is irrelevant. It is how your organization *embeds* the processes that matters. Another important point is that enterprise change management rated in every lifecycle stage and proper and effective communications and processes established with project management.

The configuration management and change management processes are discussed together because they *are* very closely linked. They describe:

- the control of all components of an infrastructure: configuration management
- the control of changes to these component items: change management

In many organizations, it has been shown that change management is truly effective only when a Configuration Management Database (CMDB) is in place and configuration management and change management operate in unison.

The term 'component' covers all items, known as 'configuration items' (CIs), which comprise an IT service. This includes source code files, objects, executables, associated documentation, test environments, system software versions, software tools versions and any other items needed to define or build the service.

From this definition, it is clear that configuration items are being written from the start of a project (eg requirement definitions), and that changes to configuration items may begin at this time. Change and configuration management functions need to be well integrated with all lifecycle stages.

The planning of these services in relation to a lifecycle model can be considered in terms of:

- controlling the configuration of a service during the development stages
- providing a definitive version of a service for formal handover to computer operations
- controlling the configuration during on-going operation and maintenance

Ideally, the same configuration and control environment should be used for all of these stages. The main differences will be in terms of the staff and organization involved. For example:

During the early stages of development operational managers will be involved with defining the requirements and specifications of the infrastructure in relation to proposed developments; if any of the configuration items in which they have been involved have to be reworked as the result of feedback from later stages, then it is necessary to ensure that the same staff/functions approve change requests.

At systems handover, the configuration items can be used to:

- formally define all components
- provide audit trails for various checking purposes
- verify that the operational service is generated from the configuration libraries
- ensure that (during operation and maintenance) the same control procedures should be applied

Separation of the service request process is also something that you may wish to consider. Sometimes these were designated 'emergency changes', sometimes 'minor changes', sometimes any other unique description that described the fact that these changes were everyday, commonplace activities that should not be subject to change management procedures. A good example is resetting passwords.

The issue comes down to maintaining and building a process that is suitable for purpose, interfacing to wider activities (project management) and also pragmatic, allowing essential day-to-day activities to proceed where that is clearly necessary.

Incident and Problem Management

Incident and problem management are functions primarily for operational services, although there is no reason why such a process should not be used in a pragmatic manner to support services development. They are used, principally, in:

- incident control - restoring normal service following production failures (a reactive environment)
- problem control - getting to the root cause of incidents so that they can be fully resolved (a more mature, proactive environment)
- maintaining a known error database
- error control - correcting problems
- management information (on the above activities)

Although problem management is mainly active during the maintenance stages, it is beneficial to define the problem management procedures required at the development stage, and to plan for their use.

The planning stage should determine whether an existing problem management system can be used, or if a new one is required. Care should be taken to identify all of the interactions between this function, related disciplines such as Service Desk and service level management, and the maintainers.

Some organizations wish to consider event management as a separate activity from incident and problem management. The need for this is more to emphasise terminology and understanding rather than a technical issue (in the same way that in version 1 of ITIL, incident management was not a separate process from problem management---the separation was made to improve clarity of purpose).

Service Desk

The Service Desk is a vital operational management service which performs the following functions:

- incident control
- interfacing between customers (end-users) and IT
- business operations support
- provision of management information

Service Desk requirements should be specified during the development stages and implemented in time to provide an operational service.

The major planning concerns of the Service Desk stem from its tight integration with many other IT functions. Consequently, planning requires the clarification of a number of interfaces:

- operational interfaces with other functions, such as problem management and configuration management
- management reporting interfaces with other functions, such as service level management and availability management
- operational interfaces with software maintainers
- the interface with software developers to ensure that the right documentation sets are available to enable the Service Desk to function

Another effect of the close relationship between the Service Desk and other operational functions is that, for some lifecycle models, the Service Desk may have to be involved at several stages during the development phases. With the spiral model, service level agreements and reliability specifications may not be determined until quite late in the development. The effect of this on Service Desk planning may be to delay production of the final plan.

There is another factor which may have a significant effect on Service Desk planning, and that is the nature of the system being developed. For example, an organization may operate a centralized Service Desk service for current services. If a new service is developed which operates through networked sites that are dispersed geographically, this service may be inadequate. There may then be a need to provide a Service Desk service on each site and a distributed Service Desk may be necessary. In this case, there will be major planning issues concerned with implementation.

Computer Operations Management

Computer operations management describes the tasks of:

- operations in providing a quality service
- operability standards
- interfacing with other operational management functions and with development
- application of state-of-the-art methods for computer operations

Computer operations management will be involved in the lifecycle in three ways:

- the provision of computer operations services to development projects
- the planning of support required for development
- the daily operation of live IT services

The provision of computer operations services for development projects will be affected by a number of factors such as:

- the development environment (for example, organizations using networked computers to develop systems, including user developments, thus reducing the need for mainframe services)
- the larger the project, the greater the demand may be on computer operations, particularly if the same mainframe has to share development and production workloads
- technology changes, when new hardware devices are being procured and used by developers

Computer operations staff may have to participate in the following activities during the development stages:

- specifying operational requirements in terms of the procedures and job control suites needed to run a service (a task they should undertake with the ITSDT)
- specifying operational acceptance tests
- executing acceptance tests and reviewing the results
- formal handover and acceptance of a service for live running

During the day-to-day running of services, operations staff will require support from other operational management functions:

  - incident reporting should be via a Service Desk
  - capacity and performance problems will certainly involve the capacity management function
  - the delivery of changes to services will involve change, configuration management and release (Software Control and Distribution - SC&D) management functions

Many working relationships will be needed to help staff maintain an operational service, and these must all be identified and planned for as part of lifecycle support.

Unattended Operating

Unattended operating describes a range of possible modes of operation, from bridge/lights out and remote operations, through to complete unattended operating.

This subject is considered to be a specialized aspect of computer operations management. It raises its own issues in terms of planning for a lifecycle support. In particular, they include:

- developing services with the required degree of reliability to support unattended operating
- designing services which require the minimum degree of human intervention in their operation

If unattended operating is to be a requirement, planning should include this aspect within the remit of the operations analysts involved with the overall computer operations requirements.

Testing Software for Operational Use

Testing software for operational use describes the major test areas of:

- systems testing
- user testing
- installation (live or business), acceptance testing

This work is performed by an independent test authority in the IT environment, and assumes that programming staff have completed their own program and other integration tests.

Lifecycle support should provide the means to bring together customers of IT services, operational managers, and software developers and maintainers, as well as software testing staff in most lifecycle stages. There should be a separate testing lifecycle which runs in parallel with the main lifecycle. For example, at the specification stage, test analysts will wish to produce test specifications based upon system specifications. As software design and implementation proceeds, so test suites may be designed and built.

An important concern will be to develop test suites which can then be used by maintenance staff. The use of different lifecycle models will affect the involvement of operational testing functions. For example, a prototyping lifecycle places the emphasis on demonstrating service functions at an early stage of development and clearly should involve customers of IT services. Operational testing may not have a significant role to play until later in development. Any lifecycle model which is used to develop a production service must enable integration of the testing functions from the stage where service requirements are agreed.

Release (Software Control and Distribution) Management

Release management covers:

- storage of authorized software
- release to the live environment
- distribution to remote sites
- implementation of the software

The ASL uses ITIL version 1, Software Control and Distribution description, but the issues are the same.

Release management promotes safeguarding of valuable software assets. It therefore has strong links with overall management regarding security policy presented in the software lifecycle support module. The priorities, as regards lifecycle modeling, will be in identification of release dates and early description of security procedures for release and distribution.

Continuous Improvement (the 'Plan-Do-Check-Act' (PDCA) Cycle)

Quality management acts as a safeguard against mistakes, reducing costs caused by waste and the need for reworking. It focuses on the need to seek improvement in performance by enabling all personnel to collectively work for the greater good of their organization, and to recognize that customer satisfaction and business objectives are inseparable.

This is central to *all* versions of ITIL.

Quality management covers quality management systems (QMS), quality improvement programs (QIP) and total quality management (TQM), involving the following areas of activity:

- QMS implementation - planning a quality initiative, registration to ISO 9001, quality plans for guiding the quality improvement process, a quality framework and the quality infrastructure
- QMS audit - feedback and checking mechanisms for verifying the effectiveness of the QMS and reviewing progress in meeting quality objectives, collection of information to assist management reviews of the QMS and the organization as a whole

- quality training - increasing awareness of quality-related issues, providing a planned approach to the security provision of training as part of a QMS/TQM initiative, and explaining the need to develop a quality culture, with quality techniques - such as problem solving, design reviews, quality circles, just-in-time and zero defects

The PDCA Cycle relies heavily on knowledge of, and embedding of, a QMS and the QMFITS book is complementary to this work.

Security

Despite its inclusion in ITIL, security management is not an ITIL process, being much too specialized for coverage within the Library's framework. Refer to experts in the ISO/IEC 27000 series for guidance. This next section, as with all coverage of security in the ITIL publications, is nothing more than a guide to be followed up.

At its highest level, security management describes the development of an organization's security policy, and application of it to information systems. In practical terms, this requires the use of a documented methodology to develop and implement a security policy.

The growing use of IT services to support a wider range of business applications means that there may be many security areas to consider. They include:

- financial security, such as check printing or funds transfer, prevention of theft
- biological and homeland security, weapon control systems, where malfunction may threaten human life, or systems controlling chemical plants, where malfunction may lead to pollution
- computer animation
- commercial security, systems which may contain commercially sensitive product design information
- personnel security
- meeting requirements regulations such as the UK Data Protection Act or US Privacy Act
- identity management and access security
- prevention of 'hacking' into an application, either internally or externally through dial-in lines
- state security (the handling of information which may possess a security classification and be bound by the UK Official Secrets Act, or similar US codes)
- data security, within application architecture, to ensure that programs can only access data which they need

Network Services Management (Information and Communications Technology (ICT))

In most respects the ITIL processes apply to networks and communications technology in the same way as they do to mainframe or local processor technologies. The domain of expertise is the difference, with it being uncommon to find, for example, a capacity planner skilled in both networks capacity and mainframe capacity.

This is not a major problem so long as technical excellence exists somewhere in the organization and, where appropriate in the lifecycle, the correct skill set from the operations side is deployed.

Service Catalog Management

Creation and maintenance of the service catalog is an activity that should be ongoing and tied to population and deployment of the CMDB and configuration management processes. The issues to consider are really those of the customer and not IT; what does your customer need to know and what do you in IT need to know to support their perspective. As with early SLA designs, providing painful levels of detail to a non IT figure is a waste of everyone's time and effort. The catalog needs to be multi level so that degrees of abstraction are present to cater for different needs.

The availability manager would use a detailed catalog of the components of hardware and software that are part of an IT service, but a consumer of those services would not.

Annex Five: Theory into Practice

Adoption of a lifecycle approach to service management is best illustrated with a process diagram, to show how a service (consisting of information, applications and technology) is designed, developed, implemented and supported. It is helpful to demonstrate how this might work with a model flow:

While most of us will accept that reality dictates that we begin a process at a variety of different entry points, for educational purposes it is best that we start at the beginning and work from left to right.
The blue bar on the top of the diagram indicates activities that occur within the business customer or external customer (if you are a commercial service provider) environment. The blue bar at the bottom indicates interactions with the technology marketplace (where companies such as IBM, Oracle, HP, Microsoft, SAP and the like reside).
Continuing through the diagram:

1. The customer requests or suggests **solution direction and definition**. This could be something as vague as 'we need a better way to connect online customers with our product catalog' or as specific as 'we want to implement SAP'.
2. This client request or expectation is then evaluated and even **designed for the required performance**. We wish to determine the needs for availability, security, the business critical nature of the application, expected performance targets, etc. These will all be input to the design within which the technology and application development teams will be constrained to work.
3. The turbulence of the external marketplace, and new and existing vendors clamoring for attention with their newest and best-yet products, is filtered into our lifecycle via the **technical architecture strategy.**
4. The technical architecture strategy is also validated and evaluated against our **current systems and expertise**. Given the time that it takes to introduce new ideas, methods and techniques, it is wise for any organization to take its existing capability into account before adopting new technologies. This is prudent not only because 70-80% of costs will be incurred while a service is in use, but also because any new service will usually have to co-exist with a substantial legacy of applications and technology.
5. The distilled technical architecture strategy is input to the **project portfolio management**. This is usually done in the context of risk, but also in terms of interrelationships between the technology needed for the new solution and existing platforms. The evaluation of design criteria is also input. The project portfolio management then

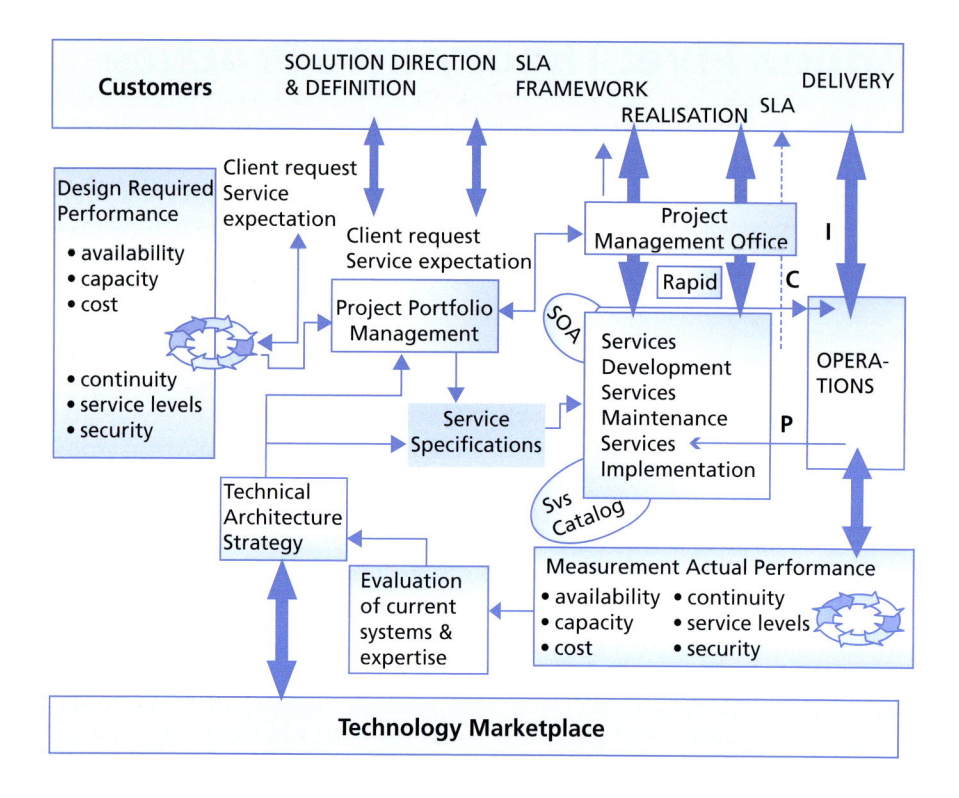

Figure 17: A Process Diagram

establishes the relative merits of each new suggestion on financial, technical, risk and other criteria, to establish a project portfolio.

6. Once a project has been formally adopted as part of the future portfolio, serious work can be done on the **service specifications**. Because it is becoming increasingly difficult to distinguish between hardware and software, and because we have had thirty years of struggle to meet service expectations post-development, the service specifications are now input into the development process for all aspects of the service: application, information, technology, etc. Another reason for this approach is that most IT organizations today are not actually involved in developing applications themselves. They are much more likely to assemble another supplier's products into a solution where their role is to integrate to legacy, integrate components and customize where appropriate to the customer's specific needs. This cannot be done well without a clear understanding, and later communication, of service specifications that affect the criteria and selection of these COTS (commercial off the shelf) or shrink-wrapped components.

7. One particularly exciting aspect of lifecycle is that by creating the service specifications in this way, an **SLA framework** can be offered to the customer before any actual work has been executed. So the customer shares a clear expectation with the IT team on what the service levels and cost will be of the new application before it is built. This understanding also helps deal with issues that occur during development, and assists the **Project Management Office (PMO)** to track progress against more than just functionality criteria and milestones.

8. Within the **development cycle** a number of processes will be initiated – V-Model/waterfall, S-Model/Rapid. The development cycle for new, maintenance or support is treated in the same way. While there are differences in speed and range of activities, fundamentally development and maintenance are positioned in a similar fashion within the lifecycle.

9. The existing **service level catalog** is considered to be an input and output to the development process, as is the **services oriented architecture**, which enables widget-style building blocks to be exploited or created.

10. The development process is under the control of the Project Management Office. This is essential, as investigations in current practice suggest that even the most rigorous **project portfolio management** fails to ensure that projects, once authorized, don't become 'zombies' (that can never be killed off once under-way).

11. Increasingly, in addition to the essential PMO activities, the integrated **change management** process is extended back, to cover the entire development phase of the lifecycle. The reason for this is twofold:
    a) while many application development groups instigate some form of change management for their development project, the experience

and even data accrued is often discarded after the project is completed and the teams have moved on, and
   b) much of what application developers term as change management is actually configuration and release management, and therefore lacks some of the essential components of effective change management best practice.
12. Once a service is complete, and after functionality and user acceptance, the **service level agreement** can be signed off before going into production.
13. Clearly, actual implementation occurs under the authority of **change management**, often executed by a release management authority into delivery or operations.
14. Once a service is operational, it is now essential that it remains viable, as the customer now relies on it for daily **operations**.
15. We continually **monitor** the service against the service specifications, measuring the key indicators as agreed with the customer, or established by the policy boards, who are governing IT.
16. The result of this monitoring is used in two ways:
   a) as feedback to the technical architecture process, as to the difference between anticipated and actual performance of technology architecture components, but also
   b) to establish whether change is required to the service, based on an analysis of incidents that occur in operations (that lead to the establishment of **problems** and known errors that need to be resolved in maintenance and support), in order to ensure that the production service thrives.
17. The incident management process itself occurs in two places, within operations and between IT and the customer, usually through a call center or Service Desk relationship.

Experience suggests that close alignment between a lifecycle process and the actual organization leads to significant improvements in effectiveness and efficiency. This often means that the organization itself needs to abandon long-held organizational structures that are built around management of the functions within technology (mainframe department, network department, desktop support, etc), in favor of structures that are geared to management around the project (design, incident management, change management, etc.).

Annex Six: References

Application Services Library (ASL), (various contributing authors) VHP Publishing, 2004.

Abrahamsson, Salo, Ronkainen & Warsta. Agile Software Development Methods, VIT, 2002.

Beck, K. *et al*. Manifesto for Agile Software Development. http://AgileManifesto.org. 2001.

Boehm, B. W. Software Engineering Economics, Englewoods Cliffs, NJ, Prentice-Hall, 1981.

Boehm, B. W. Get ready for Agile methods with care, Computer, 2002.

Cockburn, A. Agile Software Development, Addison Wesley, 2002

David, A. & B. Johnson. SSADM and Capacity Planning, The Stationery Office, 1993.

Ed. Johnson, B. and J. Chittenden, (various contributing authors). The Business Perspective on IT vol.2 (2006), The Stationery Office, 2006.

Gilb, T. Principles of Software Engineering Management, Addison-Wesley Publishing Company, 1988.

Gilb, T. Ed. G. Parikh. Techniques of Program and System Maintenance, Winthrop Publishers, 1981.

Hawrysh, S. and J. Ruprecht; Light Methodologies; It's déjà vu all over again, Cutter IT Journal, 2000.

Johnson, B. and M. Andrew. Quality management for IT services, The Stationery Office, 1993.

Johnson, B. and R. Warden. Software Lifecycle Support, The Stationery Office, 1993.

Johnson, B. & J. Stewart. In Times of Radical Change, The Stationery Office, 1995.

Johnson, B. & Richard Archer. Surviving IT Infrastructure transitions, The Stationery Office, 1995.

Palmer, S. R. & J. M. Felsing. A practical guide to Feature Driven Development, Prentice Hall, 2002.

Royce, W. Managing the development of large software systems. Proceedings of IEEE WESCON, 1970.

Stapleton, J. DSDM The method in practice, Addison Wesley, 1997.

Stewart, J., Rene Van't Veen, Arnold van Mameren. Understanding and Improving, The Stationery Office, 1996.

Yourdon, E. Managing the Structured Techniques, Englewood Cliffs, NJ, Prentice-Hall, 1979.